SO-ARX-640

Strategy for the Americas

Strategy

for the

Americas

Joseph W. Reidy

A Foreign Policy
Research Institute Book

McGraw-Hill Book Company

New York   London   Sydney   Toronto

STRATEGY FOR THE AMERICAS

51702

1234567890VB721069876

Preface

In June 1962 the Foreign Policy Research Institute of the University of Pennsylvania began a study of major policy problems confronting the United States in Latin America in response to the widespread belief among scholars, government officials, and the business community that there was an urgent need for a comprehensive review of United States hemispheric interests and policies. There already existed many "area surveys" with their descriptive treatment of political, social, and economic trends in Latin America. Therefore, the institute launched a study which would focus upon those aspects of the Latin American reality which are of greatest relevance to the policy maker dealing with the broad problems of strategy.

This study is designed to enable the reader to obtain a "strategic overview" of Latin America. Its objective is to integrate and place in perspective the many factors of the Latin American scene—political, social, economic, military, psychological, and cultural—which bear upon United States policy. In this approach, the treatment of background materials is limited to those data directly relevant to the problems of United States strategy under consideration. The strategic overview includes a probe of the meaning of major Latin American trends—political, social, and economic—and the changing power structure of Latin America. If answers to such questions can be found, the United States might identify the major "leverage points" upon which its resources and influence can be brought to bear most effectively. An understanding of the major forces at work in contemporary Latin America would facilitate a more "operational approach" by the United States in dealing with the manifold problems confronting Latin America.

The findings of the Latin American project are offered in the hope that they will meet some of the perceived needs of molders

v

of United States opinion and official policy makers—actual or potential—whether they be government officials, businessmen, or simply private citizens with an active interest in United States–Latin American relations.

The author is a North American whose views are based on the conviction that United States objectives are in harmony with the interests and aspirations of most Latin Americans. In all candor, the author has striven to evaluate attitudes and policies, both North American and Latin American, and to offer both praises and critical judgments wherever deemed appropriate.

In the process of soliciting critical comments from a variety of specialists—North American and Latin American—the author became aware that the approach of a strategic overview does not meet with universal approval. Those who favor an atomistic approach or highly specialized studies may find the scope of this work unduly broad. The emphasis placed on the human factor in Latin American development may seem excessive to those who view the process of development in an essentially material or mechanistic light. The balance struck in assessing the threat of communism in the Americas may be unsatisfactory to those who hold positions at either end of the broad spectrum of opinion on this important issue. The relative emphasis given to various segments of the United States private and public sectors—when assessing their impact upon Latin America's modernization—will be unlikely to gain unanimous approval. The idea of an Atlantic Triangle, despite the many *caveats* advanced in proposing this long-range strategic goal, may appear as a utopian vision to some in view of the complex problems which confront closer integration among the North Atlantic countries. The emphasis upon an operational approach, with its advocacy of political action, may smack of an unwarranted interjection of United States influence into the internal affairs of Latin America. The very nature of the strategic overview opens it to criticism on the grounds that it touches upon so many problems with no intent of exploring them in detail.

In no sense is this commentary an apology for the views expressed on the pages which follow. On the contrary, the author hopes that his analyses and proposals for action will generate constructive debate and stimulate further research into questions requiring study in depth.

Final preparations for the publication of this book coincided with the Inter-American Conference held in Rio de Janeiro in November 1965. It is appropriate to note that the Rio Conference of November 1965 provided dramatic evidence that the tensions and issues discussed in Chapter 6 continue to impede inter-American harmony and hamper the creation of a more effective Organization of American States.

The sheer weight of United States political, economic, and military power produces deep and adverse psychological reactions among many Latin Americans. Unilateral United States intervention continues to be the source of widespread Latin American apprehension; yet the Rio Conference failed to create a multilateral inter-American peace force to deal with continued threats of Communist subversion and other possible sources of conflict. The resultant power vacuum leaves open the possibility that the United States may again be compelled to take unilateral (or participate in limited multilateral) action in the face of a situation such as that which provoked United States intervention in the Dominican Republic in April 1965, despite the adverse effect which such action may have on inter-American relations. United States willingness to consider the Alliance for Progress program in long-range terms, and to incorporate the *Alianza* within the Organization of American States (OAS) structure, failed to assuage to any important degree Latin American frustration with the obstacles to achieving more rapid economic growth and greater stability of world markets for the region's primary commodity exports. Unqualified defense of abstract democratic ideals on the part of some members of the OAS blocked the possibility of reaching a consensus on the question of how Latin American military *golpes* are to be treated. Organizational changes of the OAS structure which are recommended in the Act of Rio de Janeiro appeared to be inspired more by Latin American pressures to reduce the influence of the United States in inter-American councils rather than by a desire to improve the effectiveness of the OAS. Perhaps the most solid accomplishment of the conference is its call for annual meetings which will provide more frequent opportunities for a productive interchange of ideas between OAS members.

In short, the Rio Conference of 1965 provided a forum for debating old issues, but the timing and the prevailing atmosphere of the meeting favored neither new nor bold steps to rectify the basic weaknesses of the OAS. A fundamental change of attitudes is obviously a prerequisite to resolving many of the inter-American issues aired at the Rio Conference of November 1965. The results of the conference strengthen the author's conviction that there is a need for a Strategy for the Americas such as that advocated in the pages which follow.

JOSEPH W. REIDY

Acknowledgments

The Foreign Policy Research Institute completed this study with the generous support of individual contributors, corporate entities, and private foundations. Consequently, the members of the institute and the author express their gratitude to the supporters, too numerous to permit individual acknowledgment, who contributed to the Latin American project.

Dr. William R. Kintner, deputy director of the Foreign Policy Research Institute, not only suggested the need for developing a strategic approach to the problems confronting United States policy makers in Latin America but also furnished invaluable counsel to the author in all phases of the project. The author owes a special debt of gratitude to Dr. Sig Synnestvedt, a research associate of the Foreign Policy Research Institute. Dr. Synnestvedt assembled much of the source material, conducted important basic research and supported project activities in other ways too numerous to mention. Chapters 6, 7, and 8 were developed in large part from the research conducted by Dr. Synnestvedt.

The staff of the Foreign Policy Research Institute was of great assistance in advancing preliminary drafts into the form which the book has now taken. The author is indebted to Dr. Robert L. Pfaltzgraff, Jr., for his organizational and editorial suggestions. Acknowledgment is also made for the constructive critiques made by Drs. Stefan Possony and James E. Dougherty—associates of the institute—and by Dr. Frank Munk, a visiting research investigator. Staff meetings conducted under the chairmanship of the director of the Foreign Policy Research Institute, Dr. Robert Strausz-Hupé, were also helpful in subjecting some of the principal themes of the book to critical examination.

A number of graduate students of the University of Pennsylvania served the project as research assistants. Working under the supervision of Dr. Synnestvedt and the author, they provided essential help in exploiting a multitude of sources. The research assistants to whom the project is particularly indebted are Carol-Lee Hurley, Herbert Folpe, Hubert Conradt, John Deiner, Edward Duane, Kay Kintner White, Dominique Raillard, and Edward Marrero.

The Foreign Policy Research Institute was particularly fortunate in having the support of consultants who possessed great depth of experience in Latin American affairs. The advice of Dr. Arthur P. Whitaker, associate of the Foreign Policy Research Institute and visiting professor at Princeton University, was extremely useful throughout the project. Merwin L. Bohan, formerly United States Ambassador to the Economic and Social Council of the OAS, provided valuable insights based on his many decades of residence and government service in Latin America. Other consultants to whom the author is indebted are John C. Dreier, formerly United States Ambassador to the OAS and now director of the Inter-American Center, School of Advanced International Studies, Johns Hopkins University; George Wythe, formerly chief of the Latin American Division, Department of Commerce; and Harold M. Randall, formerly United States Ambassador to the Economic and Social Council of the OAS and now professor of Latin American studies, School of International Service, The American University. A number of informal consultants also were of great assistance to the author. These consultants—too numerous to be given individual mention—include private businessmen, labor officials, academicians, and United States diplomatic and military personnel.

An effort was also made to solicit opinions from a wide variety of well-informed Latin Americans, some resident in the United States, others interviewed during the course of the author's field trip to Latin America. The Latin Americans who contributed comments and suggestions include academicians, economists, journalists, diplomats, and senior political figures.

No acknowledgment would be complete without expressing gratitude to those whose secretarial services are so essential to a project of this type. The author is deeply appreciative of the expert and conscientious contribution made by the project secretary, Mrs. Kay Christiansen Lee, who maintained project files, handled project correspondence, and transformed a series of rough drafts into a final manuscript. The author also acknowledges the services rendered the project by his wife, Gladys Elizabeth, who contributed useful insights into the human factor in Latin America's development as well as her secretarial talents.

The author assumes complete and sole responsibility for all opinions expressed. His judgment on some controversial issues does not necessarily accord with that of many persons whose views and assistance he solicited.

JOSEPH W. REIDY

Contents

1

Westernization:

A Framework

for United States

Strategy

Supersonic jets, intercontinental missiles, communications satellites, and manned space vehicles have shattered narrow molds of strategic thinking and wrought the geographic unity of our planet. Consequently, a Strategy for the Americas must be formulated within a broader conceptual framework than has hitherto been the case; no longer can it be conceived within hemispheric confines or isolated from United States global concerns.

The phenomenon of Westernization suggests a framework within which the policy maker can discern the major currents at work in the modern world, place them in perspective, and grasp their significance to United States national interests. The Westernization process provides a philosophical base upon which to build an increased sense of Western consciousness, and yields an enlarged vision with which the contemporary world "conflict of systems" can be placed in perspective.

Five hundred years ago, a new civilization—immensely vigorous, restless, and inventive—began to emerge in Europe from the long twilight which followed the sunset of Hellenic and Roman civilization. The new nation-states which took shape in Europe established bridgeheads on the farther shores of the

1

Atlantic and along the coasts of Africa and Asia. The spread of Westernization beyond Europe had begun. The pervasive forces unleashed by Westernization have continued in our time to exert a revolutionary effect upon the entire world. Those peoples who had absorbed most fully the impulses from a series of energizing changes—the Renaissance, the Reformation, the Enlightenment, and the Industrial Revolution—experienced most profoundly the process of Westernization.

The way of life regarded as Western—though implicit in such terms as the "open society" and the "free world"—is founded on a number of principles and values of which the following are central: monotheism, human dignity, popular sovereignty, the rule of law, social justice, reciprocal civil rights and responsibilities, basic human freedoms, nationalism, confidence in human potentials, the value of rational thought and scientific investigation, the right of private property, and the value of economic productivity and material progress.

Some Western tenets require reconciliation: A spiritual heritage has vied with a materialistic bent; the emotion of nationalism conflicts with the unifying pressures of technology; social justice contends with economic productivity. But the way in which the West has confronted these issues attests to its vigor. Pragmatic approaches have preserved ideals but added adaptability and flexibility. Pluralistic organizations have preserved unity while permitting diversity. Western pragmatism and pluralism have combined with such qualities as tolerance and ingenuity to create an unusual capacity for evolutionary reform.

Westernization is closely linked to the acquisition of political, economic, and military power. Aside from its humanistic values, the West has developed such highly efficient methods of organizing human and material resources that terms such as "progress," "development," and "modernization" are synonymous with the process of Westernization. Countries such as the Soviet Union and Japan owe much of their strength, as well as their status among the developed nations of the world, to their absorption of Western technology and organizational methods. The advancement of nations in less developed regions of the world can be measured largely by the degree to which they achieve

Western norms of political stability, economic growth, and social justice. While none of these observations justifies a Western chauvinism, they should be a source of pride and confidence in Western capacities. Clearly, Westernization is the most dynamic force at work in the modern world.

The pace of Westernization is accelerating rather than receding and shows signs of sustained creativity in contrast to the spurts of great achievement followed by regression which have been characteristic of other societies in the course of history. Western ideals have become so firmly anchored in widely dispersed regions of the world that cyclical theories of history on the rise and decline of civilizations have less and less relevance in an increasingly Westernized world. The technological revolution—itself the product of Western minds—seems to assure not only the survival but the continued permeation of Western thought. Hence, Westernization promises to exercise a continuing influence upon the entire world.

The modernizing impulses transmitted from Europe and North America have been absorbed in varying degrees by other world areas. While some have adopted in large measure the values of the West, others have "filtered" the forces of Westernization and might be described as "of the West, but with a difference." Thus, Westernization is a relative concept which cannot be defined very closely without losing its utility as an expression of a broad but variegated current in human development. The long process of Westernization has been marked by periods of stagnation, instability, and revolutionary change. Therefore, non-Western societies exposed to Western impulses can hardly be expected to absorb them fully or quickly even if they were disposed to do so. Moreover, the revolutionary impact of the West cannot be expected automatically to bring stability to traditional societies whose values, traditions, and institutions it is undermining.

Closer Western integration must logically be the salient objective of United States strategy for both ideological as well as geopolitical reasons. The creation of a North Atlantic Community is the foremost task in the pursuit of this objective. The effective integration of the resources of the North Atlantic nations would bring together peoples who share many common

values, and would provide them with a strong base from which
to defend their way of life. But even the attainment of this goal
would not give the West cause for full satisfaction. In the modern conflict of systems, victory belongs to that system which
demonstrates the superiority of its values and maintains both the
power and the will to extend as well as preserve its way of life.
Consequently, non-Western regions inevitably become battle-
grounds on which opposing ideologies contest.

The dynamics of Westernization bear heavily upon a Strategy
for the Americas. The region is enveloped by revolutionary currents. Human attitudes and institutions are in the process of
change. Latin America's problems can be seen in better perspective when viewed within the context of the process of Westernization. Long the object of Western dynamism, some areas of Latin
America are clearly and fully "of the West." However, in others
the force of Westernization has been diluted or filtered by forces
which must be the subject of subsequent examination. The impact of the modern West on Latin America has created tensions
and placed traditional Iberian cultural values under pressure.
Yet, since goals and aspirations held by most Latin Americans
are in themselves a product of the West, the region's modernization depends upon its adoption of those human attitudes, organizational methods, and productive techniques upon which Western progress has been based. It is, of course, neither possible nor
desirable that Latin America be made over into an image of the
United States or of the more advanced nations of Western Europe. Latin American nations will retain their own personalities.
The tolerance of the West for diversity facilitates a process of
cultural fusion rather than demanding conformity to rigid norms.

*Latin America's fuller identification with the modern West is
the prime objective of a Strategy for the Americas and an integral element in a United States grand strategy designed to build
a more closely integrated Atlantic world.* With this long-range
strategic goal in mind it is appropriate to turn to an assessment
of present-day United States interests—military, economic, and
political—in Latin America.

Hemispheric Military-Strategic Interests

The United States has traditionally opposed the establishment of a hostile power within the Western Hemisphere. It is this vital interest which inspired the Monroe Doctrine, opposition to Axis penetration during World War II, the Rio Defense Treaty of 1947, United States military assistance to Latin America following World War II, and the sharp United States reaction to Soviet offensive missiles in Cuba during the crisis of October 1962. The United States has based this policy upon the plausible assumption that the military presence of a hostile power in Latin America could provide avenues of approach for launching offensive attacks upon other countries in the Western Hemisphere and could restrict or inhibit United States access to essential strategic materials, limit command and control of important sea lanes, and divert United States military power from crisis points elsewhere in the world.

These military-strategic considerations remain valid today. However, modern technology and recent developments in the art of warfare have modified traditional thought on where and how United States vital interests in the Western Hemisphere might best be defended. Some areas of Latin America obviously have greater military significance than others. The positioning of hostile forces in Mexico or Cuba has always been considered a direct military threat to the United States. Central America, together with Colombia and Venezuela, has long been considered of special importance to the security of the United States because of its strategic location with respect to the defense of the Caribbean and the approaches to the Panama Canal. Consequently, United States military interests in Latin America remain strongly Caribbean-oriented, with the notable exception of the northeastern hump of Brazil—important as a terminus for an air-sea link between South America and Africa as well as a base from which South Atlantic sea traffic might be controlled.

United States security interests in Latin America cannot be narrowly interpreted, since hostile encroachments can spread from more remote regions to strategically more vital geographic areas.

Communist penetration in Cuba has provided vivid emphasis of Latin America's vulnerability to an indirect or unconventional attack. Communist subversion and "wars of national liberation" are no less menacing than overt military aggression.

Obviously, Latin America's role in United States military-strategic planning depends on the nature of the conflict for which the Americas must prepare. Events in recent years have demonstrated that the threat of nuclear warfare and the advent of intercontinental missiles have not rendered obsolete all conventional military considerations. The United States has been engaged in counterinsurgency operations requiring conventional warfare capabilities. The existence of a Communist regime in Cuba and the contingent possibility that other Cubas may emerge give emphasis to the need for a flexible and varied military posture.

The Panama Canal continues to be of major importance to the United States, as well as to many Latin American nations and the free world in general. Perhaps the Canal's utility in facilitating interocean commercial maritime traffic now exceeds its strategic importance as a link in the movement of military forces. In a modern conflict, the movement of naval forces through the Canal is not so important as in the prenuclear age. Moreover, it is questionable whether the Canal can be defended against nuclear attack. Nevertheless, the Canal's utility to commercial maritime traffic and conventional military movements represents an important strategic asset for the free world. In fact, in view of the technical deficiencies as well as the political difficulties which the Panama Canal presents to the United States, there is an urgent need to develop a sea-level canal—preferably as a joint inter-American undertaking—along one or another of the alternative routes regarded to be feasible.[1]

Agreements permitting the United States to use certain Latin American air and naval bases in the event of an actual or threatened international conflict would facilitate United States defense of its southern periphery and the command of hemispheric lines of access. These bases would be important not only to United States efforts to defend the Panama Canal and other maritime

[1] United States surveys of alternative routes, along with diplomatic discussions with the Latin American countries concerned, were under way in 1965.

shipping lanes in the Caribbean but also to the more general United States military-strategic interest in commanding the Atlantic and Pacific air and sea lanes which provide links with various points in the Southern Hemisphere, including Africa.

A number of factors have reduced, but by no means eliminated, Latin America's importance to the United States as a supplier of strategic materials. During World War II and afterward, Latin America was the source of over thirty-five strategic materials, among them antimony, bauxite, copper, iron, lead, zinc, tin, tungsten, platinum, mercury, molybdenum, and petroleum. Many raw materials previously considered strategic have declined in importance and have been removed from the critical category. Technological advances that have made possible more efficient refining processes, the miniaturization of finished products, and a wide assortment of substitutes have greatly lessened United States dependence on foreign sources. Moreover, the United States strategic stockpiling program provides a "cushion" for emergency requirements. Furthermore, even when continued dependence exists for certain strategic materials, supplies from outside Latin America would probably meet United States needs in the event of conventional warfare. In a nuclear confrontation it is probable that the United States would be compelled to rely entirely upon strategic materials available within continental limits rather than depend upon foreign supplies, whether from Latin America or elsewhere.

Despite reduced United States dependence on Latin America for strategic materials, however, the region's importance in this respect should not be deprecated. Some Latin American countries are low-cost producers of petroleum, minerals, and other products which the United States might procure in greater quantities with several advantages in mind. While domestic United States sources are available in most cases, some Latin American producers have a comparative cost advantage. Permitting greater Latin American access to the United States market would be consonant with the trade-not-aid philosophy as well as with the desirability of maintaining United States strategic reserves of certain nonrenewable resources now being rapidly depleted. Moreover, Latin America is an important supplier of some strategic items to other countries of the free world—especially in Europe—which do not possess the same degree of self-sufficiency as the United States. Finally, changing technology has given added importance to some minerals which Latin America is now capable of supplying in greater quantities.

The space age has introduced new factors which bear upon Latin America's military-strategic importance. Tracking stations in Latin America have facilitated the testing of long-range missiles and satellites launched from the United States. A variety of manned and automatic satellites or orbital systems are becoming operational. These systems require tracking, monitoring, and guidance stations. One such facility has been established in Latin America, and additional installations may be needed to improve operational control over current or future orbital systems.

The development of new weaponry increases the need for building new defensive capabilities. Latin America may be called upon to play a more important part in hemispheric defense in the years ahead. It is quite conceivable that the Soviet Union has developed or will soon produce ballistic missiles of global range. Moreover, the Soviets are known to have submarines with missile-launching capabilities, and their space technology has produced orbital systems that are obviously well advanced. It is apparent that the United States can no longer regard its southern frontier as safe or secure. The submarine-missile combination gives added emphasis to the continuing need for conventional air and naval bases. Thus, an anti-submarine-warfare capability, particularly in the Caribbean area, looms large as a major requirement to protect United States military-strategic interests.

Hemispheric Economic Interests

The line which divides United States military-strategic and economic interests in Latin America is sometimes difficult to establish. Latin America supplies a wide variety of commercial raw materials not considered strategic but nevertheless important to United States industry. Peacetime productive capacity, in turn, can often be converted to meet wartime requirements. Moreover, United States investments in Latin America many times enhance the internal security and military capabilities of Latin American nations themselves.

As of early 1965 approximately $10.3 billion of United States direct private investments has been committed to Latin America, representing about 23.2 per cent of the total United States direct investments overseas. In addition, Latin America absorbs about 17.4 per cent of total United States exports.[2] For some United States firms, continued access to the Latin American market is of much greater importance that this figure suggests. In any case, the operations of United States firms with a heavy export interest in Latin America provide income and jobs to North American investors and workers, respectively. These operations also bring tax revenue to the United States government and—perhaps most important—provide a broader and expanding base upon which United States industry, with its high volume and low unit-cost production, can build. Given Latin America's resources and desire for economic growth, its market potential is substantial. A mutually beneficial commercial exchange between Latin America on the one hand and the United States and other countries of the free world on the other is capable of considerable expansion.

Hemispheric Psychopolitical Interests

The United States has attempted to develop, together with the Latin American nations, an effective inter-American organization to preserve peaceful relations and increase collaboration within the Americas on political, economic, social, cultural, and military matters of mutual interest. Regardless of its limitations, many of which are discussed subsequently, the Organization of American States (OAS) provides a functioning multilateral mechanism for harmonizing United States–Latin American issues.

Latin American political support of the United States position in international organizations, principally in the United Nations, continues to be of major importance to the United States. Certain issues (e.g., Cuba at the time of the October 1962 crisis) have been considered in both the UN and the OAS. However, the

[2] These statistics encompass the nineteen Latin American republics as well as present and former European dependencies.

United States has strongly favored keeping inter-American issues "within the OAS family" rather than having them referred to the UN, and has been generally supported in this position by Latin American nations. This stand was evident during the Dominican crisis of April–June 1965 when OAS members generally regarded the efforts of UN representatives attempting to arrange a cease-fire as more of a hindrance to than a help in reaching a workable agreement between the Dominican contestants for power.

The Latin American voting bloc in the UN—if such a bloc can be said to exist—does not always back the United States position. Despite occasional signs of an independent Latin American line, and isolated pressures favoring a position of nonalignment, the United States has enjoyed fairly consistent and general Latin American support on cold war issues. Latin American opposition to the United States position in the UN has been most frequent on the following matters: universality of membership, greater UN activity in the field of international trade and aid, commodity price stabilization through multilateral agreements, multilateral financing of economic aid programs, and independence for non-self-governing territories of all types.

Latin American support in UN debates may become more important with time since many of the new members in this rapidly expanding organization lack experience and sophistication, particularly regarding East-West issues. Latin American support of the United States in the UN is also a matter of psychological importance. United States political setbacks in the UN on hemispheric issues damage United States prestige and influence in world affairs generally. On the other hand, effective OAS action on hemispheric issues, together with Latin American support for the United States position in international forums, increases United States prestige and influence in a way which can be helpful in solving other international political problems.

The United States has vital interests in Latin America. The military-strategic, economic, and psychopolitical components of this national interest have become progressively more difficult to separate, and their relative importance may shift with time. Moreover, hemispheric *interdependence* clearly exists and is of great importance to North Americans and Latin Americans alike.

While there is a school of thought which asserts that Latin America is more dependent on the United States than is the United States upon Latin America, this contention is apt to generate sterile debate. Degrees of dependence do not lend themselves to accurate measurement and can be rapidly reversed with changing international events. To be lasting, inter-American relationships must be mutually beneficial. Therefore, increasing the level of hemispheric interdependence serves the interest of all the Americas and contributes to the realization of the basic objective of a Strategy for the Americas: *the creation of a more closely integrated Atlantic World of which Latin America forms an integral part.*

2

The

Atlantic

Triangle

During the decade following World War II
the United States had as a principal goal the rebuilding and
strengthening of Western Europe. After achieving this objective
during the course of the 1950s, United States policy makers then
directed their efforts to the creation of an Atlantic Partnership—
a closer political, economic, and military association between the
United States and a Europe which had already made important
strides toward achieving regional integration. The strengthening
of transatlantic ties clearly remains a primary objective of contemporary United States strategy. However, United States hemispheric commitments and interests now combine with Latin
America's aspirations and dynamic progress to suggest the need
for a still broader concept of Atlantic Partnership.

The transatlantic and hemispheric vectors of United States strategic interest, forming the two major lines along which United
States influence is projected, are complementary rather than
competitive. Both are integral parts of the broad strategy which
has Western unity as its grand design. Thus, *the essence of a
United States Strategy for the Americas is to assist Latin America's more rapid entry into the modern West*. This broadened
conception of an Atlantic Community of the West gives a harmony of purpose to the existing triangular relationships of Europe, North America, and Latin America. The term expressing

the resulting synthesis of Western interests is simple and graphic: The Atlantic Triangle.

The Atlantic Triangle rests on a broad foundation. A sense of Western consciousness links Europe, North America, and many areas of Latin America, and is expressed by multiple ties: historic, religious, political, economic, military, and cultural. A historical perspective of these triangular ties is afforded by the following commentary:

> The history of the Americas lacks unity except when the story is told in terms of the great forces, mainly European in origin, which have played upon the Atlantic Triangle since the fifteenth century. . . . The mystic notion of New World unity is less a help than a hindrance to the historian who seeks to record and explain the reality of American life. What does hold their disparate histories together is the great experiences that they have shared in diverse ways as members of that "Great Society," as Toynbee calls it, which since the fifteenth century has been based upon the Atlantic Triangle.[1]

The forces of modern technology have forged new links and created greater interdependence among the Atlantic regions. The Atlantic Triangle idea, however, does not call for tightly centralized Atlantic political institutions. Realistically, the surrender of United States, European, or Latin American sovereignties to a unified Atlantic political colossus is beyond present-day possibilities. There is merit in encouraging the vision of a unified Atlantic world, but this goal is certainly a distant one which must be approached in a gradual and pragmatic way over a period of decades. Consequently, the Atlantic Triangle concept is advanced, not with the utopian hope of creating an Atlantic political structure here and now, but rather in the belief that the common interests which link the three corners of the Triangle provide a firm base for constructing a more closely integrated community of the West.

The Atlantic Triangle idea is a catalytic concept that suggests

[1] Arthur P. Whitaker, "The Americas in the Atlantic Triangle," in Lewis Hanke (ed.), *Have the Americas a Common History?* Alfred A. Knopf, Inc., New York, 1964, pp. 147, 164.

need for the closer coordination of Western efforts to meet Latin America's pressing needs for modernization. The Atlantic Triangle lends itself well to the pluralistic organizational patterns developed by the modern West—patterns which preserve unity while permitting diversity.

The merger of three regional destinies is visionary, for the path to be traveled leads beyond the horizon of our times. Yet such visions have provided the foundations for the most stable political edifices which man has built in the past. Comparable inspiration must be harnessed to strategies which will mold rather than simply adapt to human events. A truly forward strategy does not merely accept the contemporary fragmentation of the West as an enduring political reality. It does not wait for somebody, somehow, someday to provide the conditions which would make possible a union of Atlantic peoples. A forward strategy sets positive and long-range goals, with due regard for the obstacles which the objective reality poses but with even more regard for the subjective ends of national policy.

The lessons of history illustrate the price to be paid for that parochialism which cynically rejects all hope for broadening the frontiers of the human community. Thucydides tells us of the Greek city-states which, unable to vault the barrier of their narrow interests, went down in separate defeat before the Macedonians. In contrast, the Committee of Correspondence of the American Revolution, with patience and perseverance, overcame parochial interests and in the space of a few years forged an enduring constitution and federal republic. In more recent times, the progress of the emerging European Community in overcoming the narrow nationalisms of its constituent states has astounded those less given to accept the power of ideas. Thus the idea of an Atlantic Triangle, while far from prescribing the one and only path which Western peoples must inevitably follow, suggests a distant goal toward which they might work to mutual advantage.

While the Atlantic Triangle concept has a psychopolitical content, it also rests on a more concrete foundation, an examination of which can best begin with the Latin American corner of the Triangle. In a geopolitical sense, Latin America's three salient characteristics are vast spatial extension, centrifugal regional tendencies, and outward orientation toward the North Atlantic area.

Space, together with other factors, has long been a formidable obstacle to closer integration at the national level in several Latin American countries. Yet from the time of Bolívar there has been a recurrent quest within Spanish America for a broader identity which would provide a base for the "emotional commonwealth" of which so many Latin Americans feel themselves a part. Latin Americanism is an expression of that quest. The search for a broader identity has gone beyond the limits of Latin America into Pan-Americanism, an effort to develop a closer identity of interests on the hemispheric level. While it would appear that the barrier of space becomes a progressively greater obstacle as regional and hemispheric or even wider integration is considered, this observation must be qualified by reference to paradoxical developments induced by present-day technology. Modern communications and transportation have hurdled geographic obstacles in a spectacular way. A variety of links now bind the urban centers of the triangular Atlantic region of which Europe, North America, and Latin America form a part.

Modern communications and transportation are in the process of creating a similar way of life for the *porteño* of Buenos Aires, the *paulista* of São Paulo, the resident of Mexico City, the Roman, Parisian, Londoner, New Yorker, and San Franciscan. However, the dichotomy between urban and rural areas within Latin America is becoming sharper and deeper with time. In essence, space has been conquered on an intercontinental basis with greater ease and speed than on a national and regional level within most areas of Latin America. This process has been reinforced by a second geopolitical characteristic of Latin America: centrifugal regional tendencies.

The centrifugal tendencies generated by Latin America's physical environment are being countered to a degree by technological advances in communications and transportation. Yet paradoxically, these very same technological advances are now exerting an even stronger magnetic attraction between the more modern and industrialized areas of Latin America and the urban centers of the North Atlantic area. Consequently, the development of the "big void" of South America's interior continues to lag. While the development of some interior areas—particularly in Brazil—will no doubt proceed, contemporary technological trends seem to indicate that more intensive growth in South America's fringe areas will take precedence over opening the interior.

Latin America's centrifugal tendencies have impeded regional integration. For example, 90 per cent of Latin America's international trade is extraregional. Latin American common market arrangements may alter this centrifugal trading pattern to some degree, but—considering the region as a whole—the Latin American Free Trade Association (LAFTA) confronts enormous natural obstacles to the achievement of economic integration. The fact that 83 per cent of the traffic in 1959 among the seven original signatories of LAFTA [2] moved by water (almost 56 per cent of this amount moving between Brazil and Argentina) serves to emphasize the obstacles which impede *intra*regional trade.[3]

Many years ago, the geographer James Fairgrieve pointed out that in the Southern Hemisphere there is little land south of 30°S. latitude and the areas so located are "but offshoots of those of the north." Fairgrieve noted the similarity of climatic conditions and geological structures among areas of the Southern Hemisphere, and the consequent fact that production of similar commodities provided little opportunity for trade between South America, Africa, Australia, and New Zealand. Thus, while space was itself a dominant factor in limiting contact between the widely separated areas of the Southern Hemisphere, the spatial factor was reinforced by environmental factors which gave little encouragement to commercial interchange.[4] As a result, geography and economics have conspired with history to forge impor-

[2] The LAFTA agreement was signed on Feb. 18, 1960, by Argentina, Brazil, Chile, Mexico, Paraguay, Peru, and Uruguay. Ecuador and Colombia have subsequently joined LAFTA.

[3] OAS, Inter-American Economic and Social Council, *General Problems of Transportation in Latin America*, OEA/ ser. H/X. 3, doc. 18-A Corr., Pan American Union, Washington, 1962, p. 36.

[4] James Fairgrieve, *Geography and World Power*, 8th ed., University of London Press, Ltd., London, 1941, pp. 341–342.

tant links that orient Latin America toward the North Atlantic region.

Despite these geopolitical factors, prior to 1900 the stimulus for development of a Triangular Atlantic Community was lacking. While the technology of the time had already forged closer links between Latin America and the North Atlantic area, developments in transportation and communication had not progressed sufficiently to overcome Latin America's peripheral location. Moreover, throughout the first decades of the twentieth century, Latin America looked out upon a North Atlantic world which was not only disunited in its purposes but revealed bitter conflicts of interest with respect to the Latin American area itself.

Late in the nineteenth century some European powers, led by Spain and France, began to cultivate close Latin American ties. The Pan-Latin note sounded by the French press emphasized the "racial and cultural affinity" between the French and Latin American peoples. The very term "Latin America" was a French "invention." France's motivation derived in large part from its concern over the prospect of losing some of its economic interests to increasing United States commercial competition in Latin America. An added incentive, no doubt, was French concern over its ability to maintain control of colonial possessions in the Antilles and French Guiana. A recurrent note in France's Pan-Latin campaign was sharp criticism of United States policy toward Latin America.[5]

Spain, launching a Pan-Hispanic movement early in the 1890s, sought to increase cultural links with Latin American countries. The Spaniards were motivated in part by the fear that the growth of Pan-Americanism and United States military power would undermine Spain's hold on its remaining colonies in the Western Hemisphere. Spanish journals and newspapers devoted consider-

[5] A new Pan-Latin note has been struck by France's President de Gaulle. It emphasizes cultural ties, possibilities for greater commercial interchange, and the importance of Latin America's maintaining an independent position. De Gaulle's visit to Mexico early in 1964 opened this new French initiative. De Gaulle's extended tour of South America during the autumn of 1964 gave dramatic expression to France's new Pan-Latin overtures.

able space to the "Yankee Peril." Early in the twentieth century, however, the tone of Pan-Hispanism—influenced by the moderation of Spanish liberals—softened as far as the United States was concerned, and never took on the more virulent anti-Yankee aspects of the French Pan-Latin campaign.

At the time of these early Spanish and French overtures, Latin America played a passive role in world affairs. Only two Latin American nations, Mexico and Brazil, were invited to attend the first peace conference held at The Hague in 1899. Only Mexico sent delegates. However, with the beginning of the twentieth century, a number of factors favored greater Latin American participation in world politics. All nations of Latin America were invited to the Hague Peace Assembly in 1907; eighteen of the twenty Latin American nations attended. Latin America's increasing role in world affairs became even clearer during World War I when the Allied and Central Powers vied for Latin American sympathy.

Following World War I, ten Latin American countries became charter members of the League, and others eventually joined. Just as Latin American nations had looked upon the Hague Conference of 1907 as an opportunity to promote measures which would block big power intervention, they viewed the League of Nations as a useful forum in which they could air their grievances as well as gain stature within a growing international community.

New cleavages within the Atlantic world, which erupted during the late 1930s, were reflected in Latin America by a resurgence of Spanish interest in creating firmer ties. With Franco's rise to power, Spain adopted a more hostile tone toward the United States. Franco's program of Hispanidad not only emphasized the racial and cultural affinity of the Iberian peoples but also ridiculed the democratic system generally and attempted to undermine United States prestige throughout Latin America. The force of Hispanidad, however, was blunted by other developments on the international scene. For one, in the decade of the 1930s the Good Neighbor policy did much to reassure Latin Americans that the United States would forswear intervention in the style of the early 1900s. Moreover, the gathering war clouds in Europe convinced most Latin Americans that their interests would not be served by closer links with the Axis Powers which the Hispanidad movement attempted to forge.

The course and outcome of World War II greatly promoted United States political, military, and economic interests in Latin America. The strong competition and even antagonism between United States and European interests which had marked the early decades of the twentieth century gradually disappeared when the clear predominance of the United States, rather than Europe, in Latin America was established—a predominance abetted by the problems of Europe's post-World War II recovery. This change in relationships raises anew the question as to whether the Atlantic Triangle idea—however remote it may have seemed in pre-World War II years—has now acquired new meaning and vitality.

Latin America has been the object of European influence for more than 450 years. Ties of history, culture, language, political interests, and economic interchange continue to bind the two regions. Yet there is an inclination to feel that Europe's orientation toward Latin America has so weakened during recent decades that a trend of diminishing interest has been established and is unlikely to be reversed. Viewed in the broad sweep of history, this estimate may well prove erroneous. It is an estimate prompted by the rapid emergence of the United States as a world power and the relatively recent dynamic projection of United States interests southward since the turn of the century. Perhaps even more important, this estimate fails to assess Europe's "retreat" from Latin America as largely the result of internecine warfare between European nations that decimated their overall strength and reduced their trade with, and investments in, Latin America.

European investment trends, particularly French interest in developing closer economic ties with the new nations of Africa, have contributed to the view that European interest in Latin America has declined. The relative strength of Europe's orientation toward Africa and Latin America, and more particularly the degree to which these orientations are competitive, must be considered in assessing the future of European–Latin American ties.

Europe has reached no clear consensus concerning the priority of its interests in these two regions. France has heavy commitments and an important economic stake in Africa, and will no doubt press its attempt to harness the potential of the European Community for the advancement of these interests. But France has experienced some difficulty thus far in achieving such an objective. French and German economic interests differ with respect to this question. Approximately 24 per cent of West Germany's private investments abroad during the period 1952–1963 were made in Latin America as compared with no more than 6 per cent in Africa. Since the bulk of German investments abroad were made within the European Economic Market (EEC) area itself, German commercial interest in Latin America is emphasized even more by the fact that during the same period 45.3 per cent of German private investment outside Europe was made in Latin America. Italian private investments in Latin America have also grown considerably over the past decade. It is to Europe's benefit, and obviously in France's self-interest, to develop closer ties with Africa. But Europe's ties with Africa are not in fundamental conflict with the Atlantic Triangle idea, since the latter does not in any sense exclude extratriangular relationships —many of which the United States as well as Europe will wish not only to maintain but to strengthen. The Atlantic Triangle idea should not be conceived as an exclusive fraternity. The United States will continue to strengthen its ties with Japan, Taiwan, the Philippines, Malaysia, Australia, New Zealand, and other nations. Similarly, Great Britain will certainly attempt to maintain its close ties with all members of the Commonwealth. Thus, there is nothing mutually exclusive about European ties with Africa on the one hand and Latin America on the other.

European economic interests in Latin America are likely to grow at a relatively faster pace and become greater in absolute terms than in Africa. Latin American trade with the EEC has grown faster than with any other world area over the past decade. For example, exports from Latin America to the EEC have increased by about 35 per cent since the European Common Market was created while—during the identical period—overall Latin American exports have grown only 13.8 per cent. Latin America's total trade with Western Europe as a whole rose from $3.7 billion in 1953 to $5.3 billion in 1963—a gain of 43 per cent.

During the identical period, Latin America's total trade with the United States remained stable at the figure of $6.5 billion. Put another way, Europe absorbs approximately one-third of Latin America's exports (in contrast to the 18.7 per cent exported to the United States). Latin America's capacity to absorb European exports and investment capital clearly surpasses that of Africa, and this gap is likely to become wider. It is difficult to conceive of Africa as a major market for Europe's production of automobiles, radios, television sets, and machine tools. Nor is it likely that Europe will find a rational economic basis for building up an African industrial capability in the near future. By contrast, the nature of Latin American imports will be far more compatible with European export interests.

Much of Europe's current investment in Africa is concentrated in extractive enterprises. European management and capital dominate both ends of the commercial circuit. But African nationalism—relatively restrained initially but growing more extreme with time—may in the years to come regard this form of European investment as inimical to African interests. The disinvestment which has already occurred in the Congo (Leopoldville), North Africa, and former British territories is sizable. African political instability and antiwhite sentiment—already clearly evident—may increase in the years ahead. Given these possibilities, European trade with and investment in Latin America may turn sharply upward during the next few decades. Such a development could certainly be encouraged by more active Latin American export promotion in Europe along with increased efforts to attract European investors. Europeans, for their part, might spur commercial interchange with Latin America by relaxation, if not elimination, of restrictive measures (e.g., quotas, consumption taxes, tariff preferences) which now impede Latin American access to European markets.

The integration of Spain and Portugal within a growing European Community would, no doubt, provide an additional link for closer European–Latin American relations. Dutch and Scandinavian commercial interests can be expected to increase their economic ties with Latin America. The growing political power of Germany within European councils is by no means the least consideration. The 1964 Franco-German agreement to coordinate trade and investment activities in Latin America—resulting from the Erhard–de Gaulle conversations in Paris in mid-February 1964—bespeaks convincingly of Europe's increasing interest in Latin America. Finally, the tremendous growth of Latin America's population will provide a market of almost 600 million people before the end of this century—a market potential which European exporters will hardly overlook.

Increased European attention to, and ties with, Latin America need not rest on United States persuasion or an idyllic view of an expanded Atlantic Community but can be soundly based upon Europe's concrete self-interest. The Atlantic Triangle concept is more than an ideal which depends upon a vague mystique for its sustenance. It is supported by the practical realities of European political and economic interests.

Would greater European presence in Latin America work to the detriment of United States interests? The history of past United States–European rivalry in Latin America would indicate that this is not merely an idle question. Fears concerning the effect of increased European influence in Latin America are engendered principally by the belief that United States economic interests will suffer and the inter-American system of the OAS will be weakened.

The projection of European interests into Latin America obviously can be, but need not be, antagonistic to United States interests. Latin America will continue to profit from cultural infusions from the modern West—whether they come from Europe or North America. The problems of Latin American development are so vast that more European participation in the process may provide the margin of success in bringing Latin America into the modern West. Yet a significant increase in European trade with Latin American is dependent upon European concessions which will give Latin America easier access to the markets of Europe.[6]

A rise in European trade with Latin America will in some cases result in increased competition between European and United States exporters. However, if the United States is to favor the

---

[6] A triangular series of trade or investment concessions is suggested in chap. 9.

practice as well as the theory of free market competition with the benefits of comparative advantage, European competition must be met with entrepreneurial ingenuity rather than defensive reaction. Long-term United States national interests in Latin America stand to be advanced rather than retarded by the strengthening of European–Latin American trade ties and an increased flow of European capital investments in Latin America, since Latin American economic development will thereby be spurred.

There are psychological as well as economic advantages to be derived from increased European trade and investment in Latin America. While greater European political interest in Latin America is likely to accompany its growing economic stake, this trend need not be inimical to the United States. The political goals of European and United States leaders in Latin America will in all probability be generally compatible. The possibility that a stronger European political commitment in Latin America might run counter to some United States interests is a matter which calls for closer consultation among North Atlantic countries rather than for United States hemispheric retrenchment. Should such consultations fail to achieve complete harmony, sufficient ties bind the Americas to make warrantless a defensive United States attitude toward those European political objectives which it does not share.

There is no intrinsic antagonism among the concepts of Latin Americanism, Pan-Americanism, a North Atlantic Community, and a Triangular Atlantic Community of the West. These ideas can best be viewed as overlapping circles accommodating the pluralistic interests of Western peoples. Closer European–Latin American ties need not weaken the multiple bonds which the OAS and other inter-American institutions provide. The Atlantic Triangle concept does not suggest a need to abandon or even modify the Rio Treaty of 1947 or the OAS Charter signed at Bogotá in 1948. Nor does the Atlantic Triangle concept conflict with more recent inter-American agreements, such as that which created the Alliance for Progress. In fact, European investors are expected to supply part of the $20 billion to come from foreign sources in support of the Alliance for Progress. Thus, the Atlantic Triangle concept provides a framework within which Western energies and resources might more effectively be combined to achieve Latin America's modernization and fuller identification with the modern West.

To whatever degree European and United States interests in Latin America appear to conflict, the consultative bodies available to the North Atlantic Community [in particular, the Organization for Economic Cooperation and Development (OECD)] should be utilized fully to harmonize the interests and synchronize the efforts of Western nations. The United Nations Economic Commission for Latin America (ECLA), too, might serve as a useful forum in which a common approach to Latin American problems might be developed. Presently, France, Great Britain, and the Netherlands—by virtue of their financial interests in the region—are members of ECLA.

The coordination of European and United States actions in Latin America is related to but two corners of a triangular relationship. Yet the Atlantic Triangle concept must serve Latin American interests no less than those of Europe and the United States. In this connection, it is noteworthy that Latin Americans have been foremost among those who have discerned the need for, and the feasibility of, creating closer Atlantic ties.

Former Argentine and Brazilian Presidents, Arturo Frondizi and Juscelino Kubitschek, respectively, have expressed the need for closer Latin American participation in North Atlantic councils.

An even stronger plea for triangular Atlantic ties—which specifically employed the term "Atlantic Triangle"—was advanced by the Uruguayan diplomat and secretary-general of the OAS, José A. Mora.[7] The former Peruvian President, Manuel Prado, proposed to the North Atlantic Council meeting in Paris in December 1957 that a formal link be established between the North Atlantic Treaty Organization (NATO) and the OAS with a view toward strengthening the Western alliance. The proposal was received courteously but resulted in nothing more than a routine agreement for "exchange of information."

[7] José A. Mora, "Will Latin America Continue to Adhere to the West?" *The Annals of the American Academy of Political and Social Science*, July 1961, pp. 98–105.

A number of specific steps have already been taken to give the Atlantic Triangle concept practical meaning. A Brazilian analyst has pointed out that Article 5 of the North Atlantic Treaty was clearly modeled after Article 3 of the Treaty of Rio, which preceded it by more than eighteen months. Both treaty articles stipulate that an attack on one of the parties shall be regarded as an attack on all, and neither of the articles contains specific reservations with regard to the origins of aggression. The fact that the United States is signatory to both treaties provides a *de facto* military basis for the Atlantic Triangle concept. Yet, as Barreto Leite asserts, there are many who have failed to recognize the basic unity of these separate treaty arrangements.[8]

In the field of commerce, the OAS has established a formal link with the European Common Market, with offices for liaison established in Paris and Brussels. The Inter-American Development Bank (IADB) maintains a Paris office for the purpose of disseminating information concerning opportunities within Latin America which might be attractive to private European investors. José Figueres, formerly President of Costa Rica, has joined the advocates of a triangular Atlantic economy in stating:

> Western Europe should share in the responsibility of Latin American development. Historic ties, culture and trade link our republics with Europe as much as with the United States. Although we have direct relations with the mother countries, the good offices of the United States are essential, especially in coordinating the efforts of what is really a triangular economy.[9]

Latin Americans are not alone in their support for a Triangular Atlantic Community. There is a growing realization both in Europe and the United States that many Latin American problems can be approached more effectively from the North Atlantic Community than from the United States alone. In fact, some problems—such as those associated with world market fluctuations affecting Latin America's primary products—can be resolved

[8] J. B. Barreto Leite, "Integration Is Indispensable," *Western World,* July 1959, p. 3.

[9] José Figueres, "The Alliance and Political Goals," in John C. Dreier (ed.), *The Alliance for Progress,* Johns Hopkins Press, Baltimore, 1962, p. 85.

only by a closer harmonization of European and United States policies.[10] The psychological advantages of such an approach are self-evident. Latin America's nationalistic sensitivities could be assuaged by a feeling of greater association within a Western community. Latin America both requires and deserves a greater sense of participation in Western councils. The disparity between United States and Latin American wealth and power inevitably generates envy, fear, and complexes which poison the inter-American relationship.[11] A broader Atlantic Community might give greater emphasis to the bonds that unite Western peoples rather than the differences that divide them. The psychopolitical content of this objective is the "soul" of the Atlantic Triangle idea.

In November 1962, a NATO Parliamentarians' Conference recommended that private and public sectors of the OECD nations be joined in a cooperative effort to accelerate Latin America's development. In response to this recommendation, the Atlantic Community Development Group for Latin America (ADELA) was founded in April 1963 for the purpose of mobilizing a multinational private effort to assist the Latin American private sector, primarily by increasing the flow of equity capital into selective investment projects. The Ford Foundation and other private United States groups provided funds enabling ADELA to carry out a study preliminary to the incorporation of a projected ADELA Investment Company. ADELA has established links with the Inter-American Development Bank and other international financial institutions and has built a working relationship with other private groups based in Europe and interested in creating closer ties with Latin America. These groups include the International Christian Union of Business

[10] The UN Conference on Trade and Development which opened in Geneva on March 23, 1964, provided a forum for discussion of the divergent interests of the developed and less developed regions, including those of the Latin American and the North Atlantic nations. The results of this conference clearly suggest the need for greater and more effective use of the machinery established in the OECD, ECLA, and other organizations of the Atlantic Triangle area.

[11] For a fuller discussion of psychological factors impeding greater inter-American understanding, see chap. 6.

Executives (UNIAPAC), the European Committee for Cooperation with Latin America (CECAL), and the Atlantic Institute, whose headquarters are in Paris. It is also of interest that Japan is a participant in ADELA, thus illustrating the fact that the Atlantic Triangle idea should not be conceived as an exclusive fraternity restraining nations within the Triangle from developing close extratriangular relationships.

By mid-1965 approximately 120 corporate and bank shareholders had advanced over $32 million to the ADELA Investment Company, of which over $15 million had been committed to varied private ventures in Latin America. The participating investors represent United States, Canadian, European, and Japanese firms. Among the United States corporate and bank members of ADELA, 32 have subscribed to $13,750,000 of the enterprise's total $32 million capitalization. ADELA—headed by a tripartite directorate representing Latin America, Western Europe, and the United States—marks an important step toward closer cooperation among the North Atlantic nations in their efforts to speed Latin America's modernization. Finally, in 1963 the secretaries-general of the OECD and the OAS and the president of the Inter-American Development Bank met to consider ways and means of coordinating private and public sector action within the OECD nations with the Alliance for Progress. In a related move, the Agency for International Development (AID) in 1963 provided the OAS with a grant designed to enable Latin Americans to study in Europe.

Without fanfare a Triangular Atlantic Community is being built. Despite the many formidable obstacles that lie in the path of a more closely integrated Atlantic world, important progress has been made. A mutuality of interests exists among the peoples of the West. The time has arrived to strengthen this triangular relationship in order to enable the peoples of Latin America and the North Atlantic area to achieve more effectively their common goals.

3

The

Operational

Approach

The United States impact on Latin America has been impressive. United States public and private activities there—discussed more fully in Chapter 8—have produced a powerful modernizing impulse which has fostered the incorporation of Latin America into an Atlantic Community of the West. Yet the United States approach toward Latin America has been inadequate in some important respects. There has been a lack of sophistication and finesse in applying United States assets so as to exert the leverage required to move events in harmony with United States interests. This inadequacy cannot be ascribed to the pursuit of unrealistic national objectives, basically unwise public policies and programs, or the laggardness of United States private initiative.

The root of United States troubles is not to be found in *what* it has been trying to do but rather in *how* it has been trying to do it. The United States has failed to develop a realistic tactical approach to the problems it confronts in Latin America. Even the best of United States policies can be enfeebled if the manner in which they are executed is deficient. In brief, the major shortcoming in United States Strategy for the Americas must be ascribed primarily to the faulty *execution* of United States policies and programs in Latin America. The keystone of effective strategy—*a realistic operational approach* in the pursuit of national objectives—has all too often been lacking.

The Operational Approach: The Conceptual Problem

Many United States difficulties in dealing with Latin America result from a tendency to underestimate the depth of the region's problems of development while at the same time overestimating United States powers to effect their rapid solution. The difficulty is twofold: faulty definition of the problem and failure to recognize the true source of United States strength.

The United States has tended to interpret many of the problems of Latin America in a materialistic or mechanistic manner, failing to grasp the problem of development in all of its dimensions. Inadequate emphasis has been given to the *human* factor, even though it has become increasingly recognized that development is largely a matter of the heart and the mind. Misled by a faulty interpretation of the problem, the United States is inclined to seek simple, uniform, and sometimes opportunistic solutions. More often than not, the "formula" has called for Uncle Sam's opening his checkbook. Resort to this "solution" often generates contempt and resentment in Latin America and may do little to spur development.

United States strength, fundamentally, rests far less on its material resources than on the intellectual attainments and moral standards of its people. These qualities, combined with a national will and determination, have enabled the United States to transform a wilderness in North America into a center of Western civilization. The infusion of these human qualities, rather than the transfer of United States material largess, more accurately defines the problem of speeding Latin America's modernization.

Viewed in this light, the modernization of Latin America depends to an overwhelming degree upon indigenous Latin American efforts. President Johnson stated the point well when—in a speech before the Pan American Union on March 16, 1964—he said:

> Progress cannot be created by forming international organizations. Progress cannot be imposed by foreign countries. Progress cannot be purchased with large amounts of money or even with large amounts of goodwill.

> Progress in each country depends upon the willingness of that country to mobilize its own resources, to inspire its own people to create conditions in which growth can and will flourish.

While the powers of the United States to "transform" Latin America are, then, severely limited, it is nonetheless true that the United States can stimulate and contribute to the region's modernization. The question becomes one of how United States resources and influence can best be applied.

Latin America's development calls for an enormous degree of United States personal involvement, with far more emphasis on a moral and intellectual commitment than on financial transfusions. At the intergovernmental level, an increased sense of "doing great things together" is needed. This sense of common purpose must seep down into the mass of the people and create a feeling of participation in a joint venture. The psychopolitical ✓ potential of the Atlantic Triangle idea contains elements of a mystique which might contribute to this objective. Full participation of the United States private sector—business, labor, foundations, academic institutions, and a wide variety of volunteer groups—is required to transmit the "New Enlightenment" of the modern West to Latin America. The process of greater self-involvement poses some dilemmas. The sheer magnitude of the United States participation required will be regarded by some Latin Americans as "interference." Herein lies a psychological problem which must be met head on.

Undue weight is often given to foreign opinion in the formulation of United States policies, presumably with the hope of winning friendship. Strained efforts to be liked can be self-defeating. Friendship and respect are not always compatible. When this is the case, respect is usually more important than friendship; the North American mind unhappily tends to equate the two and then pursue a host of actions based on this erroneous equation. Latin American criticism of the United States is often a reflection of frustration and envy rather than an expression of deep antagonism. Latin Americans can be expected to admire the leader whose ends are just and whose resolution is firm. Prudent use of United States national power need not offend responsible Latin

Americans. On the contrary, it would provide clear evidence of a will to survive and an ability to lead.

The United States is handicapped by a guilt complex which inhibits the use of national power. Only too frequently, the United States abstains from action in deference to world opinion or in an effort to avoid the charge of interference. Unfortunately, inaction may only serve to aggravate unresolved issues which may ultimately require an even more vigorous use of United States power than would have been necessary at an earlier stage. Thus, the guilt complex associated with the use of power breeds ambiguity in the exercise of United States strength, with the danger that United States will and determination may be underestimated at critical times.

The United States has forsworn unilateral intervention, except where a clear and vital matter of national security is involved. But the Organization of American States at times has been unable to achieve an effective and timely multilateral response to vital inter-American problems and extrahemispheric threats. The belated and almost reluctant OAS reactions to the challenge of Communist infiltration and subversion in the hemisphere are particularly evident in the case of Castro's Cuba.

The strong and determined action taken by the United States in its confrontation with the U.S.S.R. during the Cuban missile crisis of October 1962 won immediate and general OAS support. In contrast, OAS efforts to reach a consensus on measures designed to effect the isolation of Castro's Cuba have been tortuous and frustrating—even in the face of irrefutable evidence of Castro's efforts to subvert the elected government of Venezuela. Finally, after years of patient prodding, an OAS Conference of Foreign Ministers called upon member states in July 1964 to sever diplomatic ties and commercial intercourse with Castro's Cuba. But even this Conference's resolution failed to receive unanimous OAS support and, as in other cases, was adopted reluctantly and only after much delay. Firm United States leadership is more likely to produce an inter-American "consensus" in meeting extrahemispheric threats than are repeated pleas for closer regional collaboration. The sluggish OAS response to the Dominican crisis of April–June 1965—granted that the regional organization was advised after the event rather than consulted prior to the landing of United States forces—also clearly revealed the inability of the OAS to react rapidly to a situation which the United States would certainly have preferred to have handled by a multilateral inter-American military force had such an alternative been available. Clearly, there is a dangerous vacuum of responsibility and power within the OAS which the United States must attempt to fill by the development of greater tactical finesse in the execution of its policies.

The Operational Approach: Tactical Requirements

The actions which give concrete form to United States policy demand more than mere routine statecraft. A United States Senate Committee concluded as follows: "We need a forward and affirmative national strategy—a clear and widely shared understanding of where we aim to go in the world and how we propose to get there." [1] The same case was stated even more forcefully by a group of retired Foreign Service officers.

> Moral leadership and political leadership depend on having a policy, enunciating it clearly, strikingly and often at the top, and pursuing it relentlessly.[2]

The United States must cultivate the art of choosing the occasions, ceremonial or otherwise, which provide an opportunity to make clear the United States position on important issues. One such issue centers on the multilateral channels of the OAS and the degree to which they are responsive to United States interests.

United States dedication to the multilateral approach to inter-American issues is sound provided it does not become a fixation. Multilateralism can be effective only if it rests upon a widely held consensus. Bilateral and limited multilateral understandings

---

[1] United States Senate, Subcommittee on National Policy Machinery of the Committee on Government Operations, *Organizing for National Security*, 87th Cong., 1st Sess., 1961, vol. III, p. 93. Hereafter cited as *Organizing for National Security*.

[2] United States Senate, Committee on Foreign Relations, *Summary of Views of Retired Foreign Service Officers*, 86th Cong., 1st Sess., 1959, p. 39.

may sometimes offer the most promising approach to inter-American problems. Multilateralism cannot be permitted to become a sacred cow standing in the path of required action when vital national interests are at stake. President John F. Kennedy, on April 20, 1961, stated—in a speech before the American Society of Newspaper Editors in Washington, D.C.—an important United States reservation regarding inter-American multilateralism.

> Any unilateral American intervention, in the absence of an external attack upon ourselves or an ally, has been contrary to our traditions and to our international obligations. But let the record show that our restraint is not inexhaustible. Should it ever appear that the inter-American doctrine of non-interference merely conceals or excuses a policy of non-action—if the nations of this hemisphere should fail to meet their commitments against outside communist penetration—then I want it clearly understood that this government will not hesitate in meeting its primary obligations which are to the security of our own nation.

Greater operational flexibility in the execution of United States policies is badly needed and can be achieved only by development of a wide variety of channels—both public and private—for taking effective action. New techniques must be developed to exploit more fully the resources of United States private enterprise in the pursuit of national objectives. To be sure, the public and private sectors are already collaborating on a number of projects in Latin America. But the potentialities have been barely grasped, much less fully exploited.

The possibilities of closer public-private collaboration are many and diverse. A single example may illustrate the point. A need exists to circumvent certain governmental bureaucracies in Latin America which have proved incapable of making effective use of United States economic and technical assistance. In some instances, Latin American state and local governments could employ efficiently United States aid funds—provided these were put at their disposal initially rather than funneled through central bureaucracies at the national level. They are denied this opportunity because national governments have normally insisted upon centralized control of United States assistance funds and United

States officials feel they must acquiesce in such demands. Alternatives to government-to-government channels must be devised to circumvent bottlenecks of this type whenever circumstances clearly justify such action. This objective might be achieved in a variety of ways, including United States governmental contracts with private organizations capable of managing a developmental project under separate contractual agreement with the Latin American state or provincial authorities concerned. In fact, the increased leverage of such arrangements might be precisely the means best suited for effecting useful changes within the central bureaucracy itself.

United States resources should be concentrated where they will be employed most effectively. Since there are definite limits to United States resources, the largest share of United States aid should go to those who demonstrate the will and ability to put it to good use. To assure that this objective is carried out, the image of the old Yankee "horsetrader" needs refurbishing. There is no substitute for skilled diplomacy which is both prudent in its choice of action and determined in accomplishing its goals. The lyricism of Pan-Americanism has its place, but so does the operational approach designed to achieve worthy ends. The United States must not consider itself to be above exercising the leverage which its national power makes possible and its responsibilities demand. Political maneuver is a fact of life on the international as well as the national scene. "Pulling strings" and "attaching conditions" are an integral part of the game. Operational flexibility must include a willingness to cut losses and withdraw support when United States assistance is not matched by the requisite actions of others. Obviously, the same tactical concepts apply to a great number of situations other than the administration of United States aid programs.

Events in Latin America continue to be molded by the relatively few. These few—increasingly coincident as time passes with the "new elite"—possess the knowledge, strength of character, and qualities of leadership required to move events.[3] The United States must make a greater effort to identify the new elite

[3] Cf. chap. 4 for a discussion of Latin America's "new elite."

in Latin America and determine its attitudes on key issues. But no Latin American political party or interest group can be expected to ally itself in all circumstances with the United States. The United States must learn to work with a variety of political factions, charting its course to accord with its enlightened self-interest.

Politically, the United States must maintain continuing contact with "every element of real power across the whole spectrum of non-communist politics." [4] However difficult, the United States must avoid drifting into "allegiance patterns" which identify its interests with this or that class or interest group, or limit its support to parties and personalities simply because they happen to be in power. The United States will be able to cope with the complexities of the Latin American situation only by flexibility of action and a willingness to work with a variety of parties or institutional groups as long as they advance the causes consonant with legitimate United States objectives.

Flexibility of United States action is sometimes inhibited by an idealism that has little reference to the Latin American reality. United States idealism is perhaps most fuzzy and misguided on the recurrent issue of how to treat with the *golpe de estado* executed periodically by one or another Latin American military establishment. There is a ready tendency on the part of many in the United States to label such events as "blows to Latin American democracy" which call for general condemnation and a policy of diplomatic nonrecognition. While it is true that such condemnation is sometimes warranted, generalizations on the question have little merit, since the Latin American *golpe* quite often serves as a practical step in an extraconstitutional system of checks and balances. In many instances, democratic and constitutional *forms* are violated by the *golpe;* but in the process anarchy is averted, civil mismanagement is terminated, and the *substance* of popular sovereignty is maintained. A more realistic and pragmatic United States approach to this issue and others is needed. Well-meaning idealism—whatever its merits—is an in-

---

[4] United States Senate, Committee on Foreign Relations, *The Operational Aspects of U.S. Foreign Policy,* 86th Cong., 1st Sess., 1959, p. 33. Hereafter cited as *The Operational Aspects of U.S. Foreign Policy.*

adequate guide to effective political action. A United States policy firmly linked to the popular will and welfare of the Latin American *people*—whatever the ruling faction and its form of government—would provide both ideological content as well as operational flexibility to a sophisticated program of United States political action.

Efforts to spur Latin American development are most likely to be successful when United States economic and technical assistance is linked to an effective program of political action. For their part, Latin Americans must look to able and honest public officials, capable of formulating sound policies and administering them efficiently. Wherever in Latin America such officials are found, they deserve full United States support. Where enlightened Latin American leadership is not found, United States aid programs must be reassessed or other means—such as, for example, private channels as discussed previously—must be opened in order to bypass those Latin American bureaucracies which prove to be either too corrupt or inefficient to make full use of United States assistance. *Effective political action must create a link between United States resources and enlightened Latin American leadership.* Until such a link is established, a variety of ills—capital flight, crippling inflation, irresponsible prestige projects, and a state interventionism which protects inefficient government enterprises or noncompetitive private ventures—will continue to plague Latin America's development as well as United States policy objectives.

Through appropriate political action, the United States must unite with those Latin American leaders who share its concern with Communist infiltration and subversion. United States "sermons" on the menace of communism have little effect unless combined with concrete action which will demonstrate effectively "the wages of sin" and "the rewards for virtue" in dealing sternly with domestic subversion. The political advantages of being strongly anti-Communist must be as clearly demonstrated as the disadvantages of vacillation on this important question. Political action must fill the vacuum of responsibility which has often thwarted OAS initiative on this as well as other vital issues.

The United States, once it identifies the new elite with which it can work, must encourage them to assume positions of responsibility. In some countries, this course of action requires the strong support of one or another institutional element or key power group. Since United States political action cannot be confined to pressing for reforms, the United States must also encourage the formation of integrative political forces within societies which often are prone to fragmentation.

The strategist must draw upon a wide assortment of techniques in his conduct of political action. One tactic might be termed "maintaining the option," i.e., avoidance of unqualified commitment to one or another faction. When the United States has made unqualified commitments in the past, it has often divested itself of needed leverage. Even if it be United States policy to support the "ins" in a given power struggle, better leverage can be maintained if the door has not been completely closed to the responsible elements among the "outs." In short, maintaining the option can provide a needed negotiating point with the "ins" and a reasonable hope for the responsible "outs."

Still another facet of maintaining the option calls for reserving decision as to the *means* by which certain goals are pursued. United States policy supports constructive socioeconomic change in Latin America. There is general agreement on the desirability of effecting these changes in an *evolutionary* manner. Obviously, peaceful and orderly change is preferable to the violence and disorder of revolution. Unfortunately, there is little to suggest that "the establishment" in some Latin American countries possesses the foresight and sense of mutual accommodation required to permit evolutionary processes to achieve significant results within a reasonable period of time. The United States should continue to encourage and support *evolutionary* change by all means possible. But—and this is where maintaining the option comes into play—it would be both tactically and psychologically disadvantageous for the United States to wed itself to an evolutionary process. Objective circumstances may clearly reveal that the rate of change permitted by a given establishment is simply not adequate to meet the need. In other words, there are, and are likely to continue to be, stagnant situations in Latin America which may require none other than *revolutionary* solutions. Consequently, the United States must maintain the option of supporting democratically oriented revolutionary efforts when it becomes clear that immobilism impedes more desirable evolutionary processes. To do otherwise might well abandon revolutionary movements to the Communists or other extremists who might then steer events in a manner inimical to United States interests.

A United States operational approach, and particularly the application of political-action techniques, will inevitably bring charges of "intervention" from Latin American Communists, extreme Leftists, and ultranationalists. Such opposition must be accepted as inevitable. Well-meaning citizens—United States and Latin American nationals alike—may also express apprehension regarding the use of political action. The reservations of the latter can only be met by logic and the building of an increasing awareness of the realities of contemporary world politics. Just as unbridled freedom can lead to anarchy, and the abuse of power can lead to tyranny, so also political action can be conducted irresponsibly. The possibility that United States political action may on occasion be pursued unwisely does not call for its abandonment but rather for its prudent use and close control.

United States political action must be aligned with the will and the aspirations of the Latin American peoples. When Latin Americans express their will freely through the electoral process, their choice must be respected as a matter of course whether favorable or not to United States interests. However, when Latin Americans are denied the democratic electoral process, their will must be interpreted by the United States and other members of the inter-American system. Latin America's modernization is the focal point upon which Latin American aspirations and United States policy objectives converge. There is no reason why the United States cannot identify itself fully with Latin America's quest for hemispheric peace, political stability, economic progress, and social justice. In fact, the attainment of these ends should constitute the essential goals of United States political action.

Ideally, United States political action should respond to the initiative of Latin America's new elite groups. But, as a practical matter, it is more likely to result from the simultaneous recognition of common United States–Latin American interests and goals on the part of the United States policy maker and the indigenous Latin American new elite. The tactical advantage of Latin Americans taking the lead in joint political action ventures is self-evident.

The dynamism of the West—and *not* the Communist scavengers of revolution—has been and remains the prime mover in our modern world. Yet the West has failed so far to develop the techniques for guiding the very forces which it has set in motion. Political action is the instrumentality by which the United States can attempt to direct into constructive channels the revolutionary impact which the forces of Westernization have had upon Latin America.

The tactics of international communism clearly reflect an understanding of and proficiency in the art of political action. Communist strategy is selective and elite-oriented. The operational and organizational skill of communism, rather than the ideology of Marxism-Leninism, is the source of its strength.

The channels available to the open society of the United States for the conduct of political action far exceed those available to Moscow and Peking. The West, by virtue of its multiplicity of human contacts, clearly possesses a superior political-action potential. If only the immense reservoir of knowledge and skills available to the United States public and private sectors could be effectively joined and oriented toward a common political purpose, United States tactical capabilities would increase manyfold. Inspired leadership must evoke the will to effect such collaboration and provide the organizational framework within which it can be brought to bear on the problems facing the United States in Latin America.

The Operational Approach: Organizational Requirements

The complexities of the modern world have merged many foreign and domestic issues. United States embassies abroad are engaged in a variety of activities which concern far more United States governmental organs than those traditionally associated with foreign affairs. Other than their expected complement of Department of State and Department of Defense personnel,

United States embassy staffs include representatives of several more executive departments and agencies. On the domestic scene, congressional involvement in foreign policy matters is increasing. Moreover, there is a growing and legitimate demand on the part of the United States private sector for a voice in the design of foreign policies which vitally affect its interests. The merger of foreign and domestic issues reflects a shrinking world of growing interdependence.

Given the many valid but inevitably divergent interests at stake, the task of finding the best structure within which a Strategy for the Americas can be formulated is enormously difficult. Among the many problems to be resolved, two questions urgently require more adequate answers. First, how can the Executive direction and control of United States policies in Latin America be strengthened? Second, how can the United States public and private sectors better coordinate their efforts?

Presidential Command

Responsibility for charting the United States course in foreign affairs rests in the hands of the President. As a report issued by the Senate Foreign Relations Committee puts it:

> Clearly, only the authority of the President himself can reconcile the various conflicting claims and pressures—military and financial, industrial and agricultural, bureaucratic and private— that affect our relations and operations in various foreign countries.[5]

A report of the Senate Committee on Government Operations, echoing the opinion just quoted, states that there is "no alternative to relying upon the President as the judge and arbiter of the forward course of policy. . . ."[6]

Obviously, the President needs assistance in charting the course of United States action abroad. The President has traditionally looked to the Secretary of State to fill the role of principal adviser in determining United States foreign policy. However, the

[5] *The Operational Aspects of U.S. Foreign Policy*, pp. 62–63.
[6] *Organizing for National Security*, p. 21.

formulation of foreign policy requires a melding of interests which is far too complex to "house" within one cabinet-level department. To cite but one example: The Department of Defense has an important interest in foreign policy decisions affecting the military posture of the United States. If political and military views clash in the formulation of a Strategy for the Americas, to whom shall the President turn for an integrated perspective which is devoid of departmental or bureaucratic self-interest? To resolve such questions, the policy-making process has depended heavily upon the staff work of "coordinating committees," *ad hoc* "working groups" and "task forces."

Unfortunately, the "committee approach"—whatever its label—has tended to substitute bureaucratic consultation for Executive direction. The "group approach" to the formulation of United States foreign policy tends to reward the cautious and penalize those who might pursue a more imaginative line of action. It frequently inhibits the flow of information between the points of decision and action. At times, it simply does not grind out a needed decision or does so only after the course of events has "decided" the matter at issue.

The National Security Council (NSC), created to resolve important questions of United States strategy, suffers many of the defects inherent in the committee approach. NSC members tend to represent the point of view, and not infrequently the vested interest, of the particular segment of the bureaucracy for which they speak. The "task force," usually created with a specific and short-range mission, represents another form of interagency coordination. At times, critical issues have been handled successfully by this method. For example, a recent innovation in the NSC's makeup resulted in the creation of the Executive Committee of the NSC—in effect an operationally oriented task force which, incidentally, performed creditably during the Cuban missile crisis of 1962. However, there is serious doubt as to the ability of the task force to function in an extended crisis or in the event of two or three major crises occurring simultaneously. More recently, the Latin American Policy Committee and a special committee to deal with counterinsurgency matters have operated quietly as interagency coordinating groups. While their

effectiveness cannot be judged on the basis of public information, it is highly probable that they, too, suffer from the defects
inherent in the committee approach.

Many of the same organizational weaknesses appear at the
"action end" of United States foreign policy, i.e., in United States
embassies abroad. Although Executive directives have made it
clear that United States ambassadors serve as personal representatives of the President, the ambassador does not normally
enjoy the operational latitude which this personal and direct
relationship with the President would seem to confer. In fact, if
not in theory, the ambassador must often look for policy guidance
and action approval to the "desk level" in the Department of
State. True, guidance can be sought and clearance for action
obtained at the highest levels when critical questions arise; but,
generally speaking, the ambassador receives guidance and action
approval from the desk officer "after appropriate coordination."

Moreover, the ambassador's freedom to manage his embassy's
staff is limited by the fact that many key officers represent executive departments other than the Department of State and are
expected to concentrate their attention on the special interests of
their "parent organization." Long-established bureaucratic structures and personnel practices stand squarely in the path of proposed reforms of this "system." The ambassador must rely on a
"country team" as the basic instrument for coordinating actions
and executing policy directives. The country team is composed
of the principal officers representing the State Department, AID,
the United States Information Agency (USIA), the military services and other executive agencies. While useful in many respects,
the country team inevitably suffers from essentially the same
defects as those displayed by Washington "coordinating committees." The country team has no corresponding organization in
Washington to which it is responsible or to which it can look for
guidance, direction, and support. Members of the country team
are normally guided by what they feel to be the interests of that
governmental department or agency which they represent.
Country-team meetings often become "mutual briefing sessions,"
while actual operations are normally conducted separately by the
individual embassy component in whose bailiwick the action

falls. Consequently, the structure of embassy staffs very often duplicates the weakness of the Washington coordinating committee: lateral diffusion at the expense of executive direction. Some ambassadors—by the force of their personality and dedication to the operational approach—make the country team "work." But their success represents a tribute to their individual ability rather than to the country team concept per se.

If the ambassador's role as personal representative of the President is to be anything more than a polite fiction, he must be given greater latitude of action, discretion to make on-the-spot decisions on a greater number of matters, increased flexibility in the management of his embassy staff, and more ready access to top policy-making echelons—including the President on matters of great import or sensitivity. Finally, he needs a modern communications system that permits the rapid referral of important matters to Washington with the assurance that a rapid response can be obtained.

Space-age diplomacy cannot be conducted with horse-and-buggy facilities. The diplomat of our times must be concerned with much more than the traditional, ceremonial, representational functions and the conduct of treaty negotiations. Modern ambassadors must be concerned with "dealing inside other societies as well as with them," and must be "mostly operators and institution builders rather than reporters and negotiators." [7] They must assume the responsibility and have the clear authority to bring appropriate leverage to bear in order to achieve United States objectives.

None of these comments warrants the conclusion that the NSC, individual task forces, the Latin American Policy Committee, and embassy country teams do not serve a useful purpose. However, the point is that they have not exercised the type of executive command and control required for an operational approach to a United States Strategy for the Americas.

Another approach to the problem of achieving foreign-policy coordination rests on the assumption that this goal is best achieved by placing the policy makers under the same roof—or at least

---

[7] *The Operational Aspects of U.S. Foreign Policy*, pp. 6, 9.

under fewer roofs. Consequently, the U.S. Department of State now houses a multiplicity of functions. Yet it would be engaging in self-deception to assume that the bureaucratic assemblage and hodgepodge of functions concentrated in the Department of State always produce integrated policies. The "lateral spread" is simply more concentrated geographically. Moreover, the heavy concentration of functions within the Department of State leaves open the problem of achieving more effective coordination between the Department of State and other cabinet-level departments and executive agencies.

In an attempt to overcome horizontal diffusion and strengthen executive command and control, United States Presidents have intermittently relied upon "special assistants." Seldom in the past has this step produced satisfactory results. Special assistants, when separated from the Department of State mechanism, have found it difficult to make the latter responsive to their views. The special assistant who attempts to operate independently of the Department risks the displeasure of the Secretary of State, who may understandably come to feel that his prerogatives have been reduced. Then, too, there is always the danger that a "free wheeling" special assistant may disrupt normal Executive Department coordination rather than improve it. The fear is also expressed that a special assistant may in time build around him a "superstaff" which might "layer in" the President, thus restricting his accessibility to the views of other officers of the Executive Branch.

The above reservations regarding the utility of a Presidential special assistant for Latin American affairs are open to rebuttal or touch upon shortcomings which appear to be remediable. A fresh approach was taken by President Johnson in December 1963. The President's selection of Ambassador Thomas C. Mann to serve in a dual capacity as Assistant Secretary of State for Inter-American Affairs and as the President's Special Assistant for Latin America obviously represented a new formula. Mr. Mann's added designation as United States Coordinator for the Alliance for Progress further concentrated within his hands great power of decision on United States–Latin American policy. In the idiom of Washington bureaucracy, Mr. Mann "wore three hats"—all of them important. Mr. Mann's functions empowered him with an authority never so clearly delegated previously.

Unfortunately, the effectiveness of President Johnson's organizational innovation is difficult to judge, since it was on trial for only shortly over a year. Mr. Mann's appointment on February 12, 1965, to the post of Undersecretary of State for Economic Affairs altered the new Johnson formula in one important respect. Ambassador Jack H. Vaughn, who succeeded Mr. Mann as Assistant Secretary of State for Inter-American Affairs, was *not* nominated to the post of Special Assistant to the President. The latter title and the important functions which it carried have apparently disappeared in the shuffle. Why? Did Secretary of State Dean Rusk feel that Mr. Mann's direct access to the President as the latter's Special Assistant reduced the Secretary of State's prerogatives to a degree he considered unacceptable? Or does there exist a tacit understanding that Mr. Mann will continue to function, in fact, as the President's Special Assistant on Latin America—as his intimate involvement in the Dominican crisis of April–June 1965 might suggest—while serving simultaneously as Undersecretary for Economic Affairs? Or were there other reasons for the President's abandonment—whether temporary or permanent—of an organizational innovation which appeared promising?

Leaving an area of speculation, a few observations regarding Mr. Mann's fourteen-month tenure as the President's Special Assistant for Latin America are pertinent. The concentration of authority appeared to have established a much clearer line of command in the execution of United States policy. On the other hand, Mr. Mann confronted an enormous challenge since he was asked—in effect, though apparently not by formal directive—to tackle tasks of a supra-cabinet-level nature from a basically sub-cabinet level post. This organizational arrangement would obviously require Presidential intercession from time to time. Then, too, Mr. Mann was compelled by events to become personally involved in the details of policy execution. This opens the question as to whether, in actual practice, the day-to-day problems of conducting United States policy vis-à-vis Latin America can really be combined with the functions of a Presidential Assistant who must have sufficient time and detachment to devote to questions of broad and long-range strategy. Clearly, a new functional and organizational approach is needed.

Responsibility for developing and executing a dynamic United States Strategy for the Americas must be shouldered by a Presidential Special Assistant for Latin America who:

1. Enjoys the personal confidence of both the President and the Secretary of State, but is personally responsible to the Chief Executive

2. Rather than creating a new bureaucratic layer on the agency or departmental level, will head a small but select presidential strategy staff which—from a supracabinet level —would not be encumbered by competing bureaucratic loyalties

3. Rather than forming a barrier which would "layer in" the President, will serve as a bridge to facilitate the exchange of views on Latin American problems between the President and such other interested parties as other executive departments and agencies responsible for activities in Latin America, members of Congress with committee responsibilities or special interests relating to Latin America, and various segments of the private sector active in Latin America

4. Rather than assuming the functions of, or exercising directionary powers over, executive departments or agencies, will concentrate on making the *existing* governmental machinery more responsive to an integrated and dynamic operational approach in support of United States objectives in Latin America

5. Rather than duplicating the governmental planning now performed by one or another existing executive department or agency, will serve as a presidential adviser on (a) the melding of existing plans into an integrated national strategy; (b) the development of an operational approach to achieve more effective execution of a United States Strategy for the Americas

6. Rather than posing an impediment between the points of policy decision in Washington and policy execution abroad,

will—in close coordination with the Secretary of State—facilitate closer contact between the President and his ambassadorial representatives in Latin America on matters of great importance or sensitivity.

The former position of Mr. Mann—Presidential Special Assistant—met many of the criteria outlined above. However, to focus upon one major reservation, there is reasonable doubt as to whether the potential of the United States private sector—an extremely important element in the United States response to the challenge of Latin America's problems—can be harnessed to United States official efforts by a government official who must concern himself with the intricacies of day-to-day policy. In any case, the question of utilizing the potential of the private sector to better advantage in the pursuit of United States national objectives merits further examination.

Integrated Response: Proposal for a Latin American Strategy Board

The lateral spread which characterizes the process of United States foreign-policy making presents a paradox. Despite its labyrinthian ways, the process rarely leaves the executive branch. There is inadequate congressional participation in the councils of foreign-policy formulation. This results not only in the failure to collect a variety of viewpoints that may prove useful but also in the frequent undoing of executive plans. As Senator Fulbright has said, "Congress has neither the authority nor the means to conduct American foreign policy but it has ample power to implement, modify or thwart executive proposals." [8]

No less conspicuous is the failure to consult fully with elements of the United States private sector which are in a position, and are often called upon, to advance United States objectives in Latin America. A fresh approach is needed. There is much to suggest that a better understanding and coordination between public and private sectors might be achieved by the creation of a consultative group which might be called the Latin American

[8] As quoted by Frederick G. Dutton, "Cold War between the Hill and Foggy Bottom," *The New York Times Magazine*, Sept. 15, 1963, p. 93.

Strategy Board (LASB). The Board's membership and direction
should be determined by the President himself upon the advice
of public and private sector officials most intimately concerned
with the advancement of United States national objectives in
Latin America.

The LASB would *not* be expected to serve as a decision-
making organ, for in this capacity it would quickly succumb to
all the defects of the governmental coordinating committees discussed previously. However, such a Board might promote better
understanding of United States national objectives among private groups, appeal more effectively for private support of public
policies as well as reciprocal governmental support of private
interests, and develop the multiple public-private channels
needed to give United States foreign policy greater operational
flexibility.

Broad collaboration of the United States private sector would
be essential to the LASB's effective functioning. Representatives
of the United States private sector should *themselves* take the
initiative to form, where they do not already exist, small but
select committees to represent their views and interests in LASB
deliberations. Representatives of both the International Executive Service Corps and the Council for Latin America would
appear to be ideally suited to perform this useful function for
an important segment of United States private business. The
United States representative to ORIT (Organización Regional
de Trabajo) and the director of the American Institute for Free
Labor Development would be logical spokesmen for United
States labor.[9] Permanent committees representing private foundations and academic institutions most active in Latin America
should also participate in consultations of the LASB. Special
committees representing other elements of the private sector
(e.g., religious institutions, volunteer groups, the communications industry, etc.) might be formed to meet specific needs.

It may appear that the LASB concept would assume the form
of a "bureaucratic monstrosity," combining many conflicting in-

[9] These organizations, among others, are discussed in chap. 8 in connection
with an assessment of the United States private sector's impact on Latin
America's development.

terests in unwieldy and interminable discussions unlikely to result in a clear consensus. Should the proposed LASB take on
such a character, it would most certainly have a short life. Unless
it were moved by the spirit of intergovernmental and public-
private cooperation, bureaucratic arteriosclerosis would undoubtedly bring about its demise. The need for plenary sessions of the
LASB would be rare, perhaps serving their principal purpose as
"springboards" for major United States policy pronouncements
made by the President himself. Normally, the LASB would function on a more or less informal and *ad hoc* basis, its discussions
centering on specific problems requiring the presence of "now
this" and "now that" portion of the Board's membership. Much
of its most important work would take place within the constituent committee elements of the LASB, many of which already exist, but are in need of a focal point at which their views
can be brought to bear, others of which would form without
governmental initiative if it were felt that their views were
genuinely sought and might have some influence on the course
of United States policy.

The LASB is not conceived as another bureaucratic "giant"
but rather as an instrumentality for across-the-board coordination of United States public-private actions in Latin America.
No forum is now available for accomplishing this important task.
Thus, rather than duplicating bureaucratic approaches to the
problem of giving United States actions in Latin America greater
flexibility, the LASB would be dedicated to seeking imaginative
operational solutions.

United States policies in Latin America—however soundly
conceived and formulated—will fail unless the United States
develops a truly operational approach in the pursuit of its national objectives. To summarize, the ingredients are these: new
and realistic concepts regarding the use of national power,
greater tactical flexibility in the execution of United States policies and programs, an organizational structure at the highest
level of United States government which concentrates on a
broad and long-range United States Strategy for the Americas,
and public-private teamwork dedicated to the advancement of
United States interests.

4

Background

for

Decision

The policy maker faces the formidable task of harmonizing United States national goals—subjectively conceived as they must be—with the Latin American reality which is not only foreign but highly complex. An appreciation of the enormity of this task is the beginning of wisdom for both the policy maker and his critic. Such an understanding can best be achieved by probing the Latin American reality for those background factors most relevant to the formulation of a Strategy for the Americas.

Latin American Diversity

Latin America contains twice the area of Europe and two and one-half times that of the continental United States. The 7,000 miles which separate the United States–Mexican border and Cape Horn are marked by sharp geographical and ethnic differences.

Latin America's topography, climate, soil, geology, and vegetation vary widely. The rich agricultural resources and valuable mineral resources found in some areas contrast with the poor resources and major environmental obstacles to development found in other areas. The very pattern of Latin America's development displays significant contrasts. A sharp urban-rural dichotomy is characteristic of most nations. Urban centers around which development has concentrated are in their greater majority on or near coastal areas. The few major cities located as far as 100 to 200 miles from the sea are, with few exceptions, ocean-oriented. Interior areas constitute the most undeveloped part of South America. The greatest of these—what might aptly be termed the "great void"—is centered in the tropical forests of the Amazon Basin, an area of 2.7 million square miles (two-fifths of South America's land surface) but containing less than 2 million people. Improvements in transportation during recent decades have begun to alter the isolation of many interior areas. Nevertheless, the dominant pattern remains one of concentration of population and development in the fringe lands of Latin America. Thus, commerce between the nations and regions of the area has traditionally been by sea rather than by road or railway. The ocean-oriented or centrifugal pattern of Latin American geography has combined with major physical obstacles to overland commerce and communications to reinforce another of Latin America's prominent features: ethnic diversity.

The three major strands of Latin America's cultural weave are the American Indian, the African Negro, and the European Iberian.[1] Important differences are found not only between but also within these three major ethnic groups, thus emphasizing the human diversity of Latin America.

The Indian cultures of Latin America range from the primitive tribes of the Amazon to the complex civilizations which the Spanish conquerors found in Peru and Mexico. Similarly, the Negro has varied considerably in skills, attitudes, and customs, depending upon his African tribal origins. Even the Iberian was far from a homogeneous addition to Latin America's human composite, since the many alien infusions into Spain and Portugal—that of the Moslem Moor being particularly important—produced regional differences which, in turn, were reflected in

[1] A flow of non-Iberian European immigration, joined by smaller additions of Oriental and Near Eastern immigrants, has added to an already varied ethnic composite especially since the last quarter of the nineteenth century. The significance of this flow—especially important in Argentina, Uruguay, southern Brazil, Chile, and other scattered localities—is considered subsequently.

Latin America. A significant degree of intermingling produced large elements of mestizos and mulattoes, thus adding to an already complex ethnocultural mosaic.

Cultural Factors in Perspective

Geographic and ethnic diversity has posed major obstacles to the development or modernization of Latin America. Clearly, it complicated immensely the formation of cohesive national societies and impeded regional integration. Cultural and historic factors also contributed to the languid pace of Latin American progress during the first four centuries following the conquest.

The Iberian culture has provided Latin America with its strongest integrative element. Before its penetrating force the Indian and Negro sometimes retreated at the price of physical isolation. More often, however, he adapted to or absorbed, in varying degrees, the value systems of the Iberian. The process of cultural fusion was facilitated by the fact that all three cultural strands shared some cultural values in their substance if not in their form, e.g., authoritarian traditions, stratified social structures, and paternalistic relationships. More significantly, when faced with a conflict of values, the mestizo and mulatto generally have opted in favor of the Iberian culture. Thus— granting the significant effect of other cultural stimuli, particularly in and around major urban centers—the pervasive force of Iberian culture continues to influence the evolving attitudes and structures of Latin America.

Paradoxically—along with its many positive and admirable values and its integrative role—Iberian culture has exhibited certain characteristics which have retarded Latin America's development. Resistance to change and an arrested sense of mutual accommodation are two salient Iberian attitudes.[2]

---

[2] The five cultural values in the discussion which follows are examined, along with others, in an essay by John P. Gillin. Gillin spoke of them as middle-class values but not in any exclusive sense. It is clear from other studies that the attitudes which flow from these values are widely held by all social strata within the Iberian cultural family. For a fuller discussion of this topic see "Some Signposts for Policy," *Social Change in Latin America Today:*

The Iberian value of personal dignity stresses the uniqueness of the individual *persona*. The Iberian *persona* is valued because he is unlike anyone else and merits respect because of his inner worth regardless of his economic or social status. This concept of personal dignity does not support egalitarian notions of equal rights and opportunity, but is frequently manifested in an inordinate sense of pride and individualism. Carried to extremes, this value degenerates into *personalismo*, which has been described as "an exaltation of the I, which does not perceive itself as a unit in the group, but as the whole group itself. Pride and *dignidad* are exaggerated, and the group serves as a pedestal for the self." [3] Another derivative of the value of personal dignity is termed *machismo* and is manifested by the man possessing valor, firmness, and strength. Thus, in Iberian culture, the essentially positive value of personal dignity often degenerates into traits which inhibit teamwork, community action, political stability, and joint economic endeavor. Obviously, *personalismo* and *machismo* can also contribute to authoritarian tendencies.

A second Iberian value, family cohesion, has the positive effect of binding closely together the members of a kin group whose welfare is of intimate mutual concern. On the other hand, extreme family-centric attitudes militate against the development of extra-family community action and the impersonal demands of modern civic organizations and economic enterprises.

A third Iberian value is expressed in respect for the hierarchical structure of a stratified society. The *patrón* system prescribes reciprocal rights and obligations at all levels of a stratified social structure. While this value tends to knit together disparate elements of a society with many centrifugal tendencies, it also impedes social mobility and more dynamic economic attitudes and organizations.

A fourth Iberian value establishes tangible, real property as the measure of wealth and success. Thus, large landholdings are valued, whereas intangibles such as bonds, stocks, copyrights,

Its Implications for United States Policy, Richard N. Adams et al., Harper & Brothers, for the Council on Foreign Relations, New York, 1960, pp. 14–62.

[3] Alfredo Pérez Guerrero, *Ecuador, Casa de la Cultura Ecuatoriana, Quito*, 1948, p. 74, as quoted in Gillin, *op. cit.*, p. 30.

and patents hold less interest. Obviously, this attitude retards the capital-formation and investment processes essential to a vigorous private-enterprise system and rapid economic growth.

Transcendentalism, a fifth Iberian value, displays some positive features along with many retarding ones.[4] Latin Americans imbued with this value have manifested minimal interest in scientific and technical pursuits or in systematic and empirical investigation. Education is conceived more as a civilizing process ✗ than as a preparation for productive enterprise. Thus, many Latin Americans tend to prefer prestige positions in government, the military, law, and the arts, but the professions of the engineer, industrialist, and entrepreneur have held little attraction. Iberian transcendentalism promotes idealistic projects but frequently does not inspire the practical action required for their realization.

These Iberian cultural values have been subjected to pressures for change in Latin America. Foreign stimuli have wrought important cultural alterations in some regions. However, perhaps the most important pressure for cultural transition is the growing recognition within Latin America itself that there is a conflict between traditional attitudes and the professed goals of political stability, economic growth, and social justice.

The Iberian powers, over the three centuries of their colonial rule in the Americas, had declined measurably as compared with the growing dynamism exhibited in other countries of Western Europe. The revolutionary changes which shaped the modern

[4] The cultural contacts between Latin America and the countries of the North Atlantic area would be mutually more beneficial if approached in the spirit of a true interchange and mutual exposure to differing values. The process is by no means a "one-way street" in which Latin Americans are always the recipients and never the donors of useful cultural values. North Americans among others could profit by absorbing some of the positive features of the Latin American's transcendentalism—with the charm, grace, devotion to contemplation, developed sense of aesthetics, versatility, and ease of living which this value encourages. Latin America has much of value to transmit as well as to adopt from others. Positive aspects of the value of transcendentalism is a case in point. In the age of cybernetics, the modern West must discover ways to find satisfaction in life without the constant frenetic activity that regards labor as the supreme virtue.

West were not fully shared by the Iberian peoples. The spirit of independent inquiry that accompanied the Reformation, the liberal political currents that generated the democratic revolutions in England, the United States, and France, the growth in scientific interest and technology that brought the Industrial Revolution—these and other dramatic changes presaged the emergence of a new and advanced, industrialized and technological society in the West. Spain and Portugal did not fully absorb these energizing impulses. Their relative stagnation, as compared to the creative forces generated in other countries of Western Europe, inevitably retarded Latin America's development.

The history of the Iberian conquest in the New World and the three centuries of colonial rule which followed were not barren of dramatic and positive accomplishments. However, there was much in Latin America's colonial heritage which impeded the area's development. The colonies had little or no experience in the practices of representative government or the art of public administration. For example, of 170 viceroys appointed during the three centuries of Spanish rule, only four were born in the Americas.[5] A hierarchical and highly stratified social structure was another colonial legacy. While this structure was not absolutely rigid, social immobility characterized colonial life. Educational opportunities were severely limited. Throughout three centuries of colonial rule not a single university was established in Brazil. While ten major and fifteen minor universities were founded in Spanish America, their dominance by the clergy resulted in the neglect of studies of scientific developments and new philosophical trends. Even after the Bourbon reforms of the eighteenth century, the influence of the Enlightenment passed through an Iberian "filter," and "useful knowledge was often promoted for the very purpose of fortifying the political and social status quo."[6]

The lack of technical skills and entrepreneurial spirit inhibited

[5] Hubert Herring, *A History of Latin America*, Harper & Brothers, New York, 1961, p. 83.

[6] Arthur P. Whitaker (ed.), "The Dual Role of Latin America in the Enlightenment," *Latin America and the Enlightenment*, 2d ed., Cornell University Press, Ithaca, New York, 1961, p. 6.

economic development in the colonies. The tradition of large
landholdings in rural areas produced a comfortable life for the
favored few but mere subsistence for the many. Agrarian productivity lagged, since land was valued more as a symbol of
prestige than for its productive potential. Spanish commercial
policies also retarded economic growth. Restrictive controls
channeled commerce through a few designated ports. Intra-
regional trade between the American colonies was not legally
permitted until late in the colonial period. Moreover, the political and economic decline of Spain itself adversely affected the
development of Latin America.

The struggle for independence in Spanish America was protracted (1810–1825) and destructive. For most areas of Spanish
America, the wars of independence ushered in a prolonged
period of political turmoil, economic stagnation, and social dis-
integration. The general expulsion of Iberian-born *peninsulares*
who had supported the crown led to the disruption of commerce
and loss of needed administrative talent. Only after many decades were political order and normal economic activity restored.

Thus, by early in the nineteenth century, Latin America had
shed its colonial bonds. If measured by the human and material
standards of the more dynamic areas of the West, however,
Latin America had slipped into the ranks of the underdeveloped
areas of the world. As was true of the Iberian homelands, Latin
America came to be regarded as "of the West, but with a difference."

Characteristics of Change in Latin America

One of the dominant characteristics of change in Latin America has been its dependence upon foreign models and impulses.
Generally speaking, Latin America has been the recipient rather
than the initiator of change. Sparks of indigenous inspiration
have embellished and adapted imported concepts and methods
but have rarely created new ones.[7]

[7] José Luis Romero, *Las Ideas Políticas en Argentina,* Fondo de Cultura
Económica, Mexico City, 1946, pp. 9–10. For other interpretations of this
point see Eugenio Pereira Salas, "The Cultural Emancipation of America,"

European and North American constitutions and republican ideals provided the inspiration for Latin American Creole leaders once independence was achieved. Foreign capital, organizational talent, and technical skills combined to spur the area's economic development from the mid-nineteenth century on. European immigration added still another stimulus which was particularly influential in Argentina, Uruguay, and southern Brazil. These external impulses supported, if they did not in fact induce, other important changes such as greater social mobility, urbanization, and industrialization.

The ideals and forms of the modern West were adopted more readily than the practices and attitudes required to give them effect. The Spanish crown's authoritarian rule was followed by similar patterns established by the Creole aristocracy. The force of *personalismo* hampered development of effective political parties and led to emphasis upon individual action by the *caudillo*. Constitutions and republican forms were in most areas incompatible with the turbulence which prevailed in many countries for decades following the wars of independence. The *golpe de estado* proved to be a common means of transferring power.

The superficiality and blandness characterizing the Latin American process of change have been particularly evident in the social changes which have occurred over the years. Generally speaking, social changes have been characterized more by shifts in status, occupational roles, and income levels rather than by an alteration in basic human attitudes. The Latin American has traditionally been a conservative. He has resisted rapid and profound change and has frequently directed his energies more toward reestablishing the old order in new hands instead of effecting a fundamental reordering of society.

One of the major impediments to a more rapid and profound process of change in Latin America has been the general inadequacy of the educational systems. As late as 1960, illiteracy in Latin America stood at approximately 44 per cent, with wide

---

in UNESCO, *The Old and the New World: Their Cultural and Moral Relations,* UNESCO, Paris, 1956, p. 110. Also note Paulo de Berredo Carneiro, "The Heritage of Columbus," *ibid.,* p. 117.

variations from country to country. Educational staffs, curricula, and physical facilities—qualitatively as well as quantitatively—are woefully inadequate in most areas. Crash programs launched to deal with Latin America's educational deficiencies, while laudable in intent, have frequently not kept pace with a rapidly expanding population. It has become increasingly evident that the qualitative achievement of a given country's educational system cannot be advanced much beyond its general level of development.

The *latifundia* system, which created a relatively closed socioeconomic unit dedicated more to supporting the landowner's way of life than to agrarian productivity, has greatly retarded the process of change in rural Latin America. This traditional agrarian structure has done little to stimulate commercial interchange or to develop communications. Since the *latifundia* system also tended to depress rural incomes, it severely limited market possibilities for urban-based industries.

Adverse psychological reactions to foreign impulses pose a major impediment to dynamic change in Latin America. This reaction often takes the form of extreme nationalism and xenophobia. A "culture clash" inevitably accompanies Latin America's closer integration into the modern West.[8] Faced with the painful choice of retreat from the modern West or adoption of modern Western cultural values, Latin Americans have developed a cultural schizophrenia which Tannenbaum has described as follows:

> They value greatly all that a "patronal" and aristocratic society has given them—the ease, the unhurried life, the indifference to great wealth, the presence of many servants to make life comfortable and secure, the romantic notion of a heroic past and the

[8] The classic statement of this cultural clash is contained in *Ariel*, a book written in 1900 by an Uruguayan, José Enrique Rodó. The spirit of Ariel represented an expression of Latin America's appreciation of life's fine values. The contrasting spirit of Calaban represented the utilitarian North American —a product of passion for work who exhibits admirable efficiency but an unfortunate preoccupation with the material and the immediate reality. While Rodó's *Ariel* is out of tune with the contemporary Latin American quest for modernization, certain elements of *arielismo* persist.

encouragement of friendships and versatility. All of this they would keep. But they also want, or think they want, what the modern world has to offer—modern cities, automobiles, airplanes, factories, the latest products of science, and the gadgets of the day. They would have the best of the two worlds—the patronal, *señorial* society and the egalitarian and industrial one—and refuse to recognize that they cannot have both.[9]

Latin America's experience lends credence to the observation that alien ideas and institutions cannot simply be transplanted and expected to thrive. They must be grafted on a Latin American cultural plant. Long under the influence of foreign impulses, Latin America is attempting to find itself. It seeks its own forms through more skillful adaptation of foreign ideas and institutions to Latin American needs.

Quest for Leadership

The problem of Latin America's modernization is, in large part, one of generating from *within* those human attitudes and practical aptitudes needed to effect profound and rapid change. But change is but one component of the overall progress of development. Change per se has not always advanced Latin American development when not accompanied by another ingredient: national cohesion built upon a sense of mutual accommodation and a broad consensus as to common goals. A will to change and the spirit of national cohesion are closely related and interdependent components of development.

To force the process of change without a commensurate increase in national cohesion could, under circumstances prevailing in many countries of Latin America, engender disorder rather than progress. In brief, increased emphasis on creating greater national cohesion may be more effective in some instances in speeding Latin America's modernization than strong pressures for rapid change.

Nationalism has provided an integrative ideology which few other elements in Latin American society have furnished. But

[9] Frank Tannenbaum, *Ten Keys to Latin America*, Alfred A. Knopf, Inc., New York, 1963, p. 135.

nationalism is an emotional force which must be oriented to achieve positive and constructive ends. Herein lies a *central problem of Latin American development: the quest for enlightened leadership capable of generating dynamic change while at the same time creating greater national cohesion.*

What are the groups in Latin America that might provide such enlightened leadership? Traditional institutions such as the church and the military? Intellectuals and students acting jointly within the matrix of the university? Organized labor or political parties? New social elements such as the modern upper groups or emerging middle sectors? Business entrepreneurs or other professional groups?

The Church

The church's loyalty to the Spanish crown during the struggle for independence resulted in a grave weakening of its position. Its most able leaders, most of whom were Iberian-born, were expelled along with other *peninsulares.* Anticlericalism became a common feature of Latin American politics. The passive attachment of many of its followers debilitated the church's influence. Pope Pius XII initiated a study in 1954 which revealed that 30,000 priests, many of them inadequately trained, were tending to 150 million Latin Americans, most of whom were only nominally Catholic. This is a ratio of 1:5,000 as compared with 1:700 in the United States.[10] Even today church authorities label Latin America as "missionary country."

Although long identified with political conservatism and defense of the *status quo,* liberalization and invigoration of the church in some countries have demonstrated more recently that Catholicism in Latin America need not be synonymous with resistance to social and economic change. Spurred on by papal encyclicals, some church leaders have become champions of social and economic reforms. Church influence has grown in the universities, labor unions, peasant leagues, and Christian Democratic political parties. Catholic action groups have taken active

[10] John Scott, *"How Much Progress?" Time Magazine Special Report,* 1963, p. 120.

roles in supporting reform measures enjoying wide popular support.

The church's "new look" on key issues, however, is sharply opposed by more conservative elements of the hierarchy. A church consensus cannot be said to exist—certainly not on a regional scale, and not even on the national level in many countries. Consequently, while the church forms one of the great emotional common denominators of the region, its impact from country to country continues to vary greatly. As a generalized and long-range forecast, the church's influence as a factor for change and the development of national cohesion appears to be on the upswing. However, even in areas in which it is likely to exercise an increasingly positive function, it seems destined to play a supporting rather than a leading role.

The Military

For reasons peculiar to Iberian history and tradition, the Latin American military has traditionally conceived of its role in ambitious terms. With the chaotic conditions that followed the independence movements in Latin America, a trend of *caudillismo* led to frequent *golpes* and established in many nations a tradition of military intervention in governmental affairs. Sometimes the military was motivated purely by a lust for power, but not infrequently its intervention was more the result rather than the cause of unstable political institutions. Even if the regular military had not existed, there were many chaotic situations which left a power vacuum that would probably have been filled by one or another armed insurgent band.

Throughout most of the nineteenth century, the Latin American military became identified with the political *status quo* and the interests of the Creole landowning elite. Changes associated with urbanization, immigration, emergence of the middle sectors, growth of industry, and the beginnings of organized labor inevitably influenced Latin American military attitudes. A rising sense of professionalism accompanied these changes. The officer corps was drawn more and more from the middle sectors, while noncommissioned officers were recruited increasingly from lower-income groups. The shift in social origins of its key personnel gradually led the military to identify its interests with the social strata from which it came.

The continued political power of the Latin American military is indicated by the fact that, as recently as January 1957, military men were serving as presidents in nine of the twenty Latin American countries. While there was a sharp reaction against the military's political dominance after 1957, the early 1960s have witnessed a resurgence of military-engineered *golpes*. Many, however, have been inspired by more complex motivations than was typical of military *golpes* of earlier years.

During the twentieth century the traditional role of the Latin American military as defenders of national frontiers has been greatly reduced. Changing technology of modern warfare, more-over, makes it unlikely that they will be called upon to engage directly in a future world conflict. However, providing for internal security is a major and continuing task of the military in some countries. The cost of maintaining a military establishment has pressured Latin American armed forces into assuming more clearly positive and constructive functions which contribute to national development. Significantly, the military services in many areas have demonstrated a growing willingness to assist in promoting social and economic reforms.

Ironically, the determination to play a more active part in spurring Latin America's modernization has provided both the motivation and the rationale for some recent *golpes*. The growing trend of what has been termed *nasserismo* is usually associated with younger officers motivated basically by the desire to speed the process of social and economic change. While it has no international links, the foreign model which appeals to Latin America's *nasseristas* is evident from the term itself. The actions it inspires are almost always strongly nationalistic and frequently incline toward statist solutions in the economic sphere and authoritarian political patterns. Still another group among the Latin American military shares in varying degrees the modernization goals of the *nasseristas* but prefers to pursue these ends through democratic processes and a more energetic and positive military role. This role is frequently described in terms of "nation building" and "civic action"—i.e., activities which cover a wide range of public works generally similar to those undertaken by the United States Army Corps of Engineers, such as transportation, irrigation, reforestation, health and sanitation projects. The same programs also stress the training of recruits in skills that contribute to national development.

The range of Latin American military opinion is far greater than can be explored in this brief analysis. However, the military in most nations of Latin America will continue to play an important role in shaping the national policies of their respective countries. Military *golpes* with widely differing motivations will continue to occur. More often, the Latin American military will resort to "backstage" measures to influence national events. On balance—and as a broad generalization in an area of great diversity—the Latin American military is likely to play an important role in supporting the forces of modernization. However, rarely—except for brief, emergency situations—does the military appear capable of exercising the sole integrative role.

Intellectuals and Students

Intellectuals and students form separate and important segments of Latin American society which—while not identical in their membership—overlap within the matrix of the university. Within the university the intellectual and student join in a tandem relationship which has demonstrated important capabilities for political action. In this tandem relationship the intellectuals and students have considerable potential.

The intellectuals and students of Latin America exercise a leadership role which far exceeds that of their North American counterparts. The intellectual enjoys great prestige in Latin American society. He formulates ideas and generates ideological currents. Not satisfied with being a mere expositor, he frequently becomes a political activist with a point of view to expound and a cause to defend. The intellectual on many occasions has sought and gained political office, occupied key posts in the communications media, or held other positions which have enabled him to influence public opinion. Consequently, even when he does not assume direct leadership in politics, the intellectual's indirect influence is often great.

Student idealism and energy give impetus and follow-through to the intellectual's views. The intellectual-student link is formed in the university but often is effective well beyond this period of contact, particularly since the Latin American student frequently becomes a member of the elite within his society. The dynamism of the intellectual-student tandem is enhanced by the autonomy which Latin American universities customarily enjoy, the freedom of action traditionally allowed the student, the public sympathy which a student often evokes, and the proclivity the student displays for political action. The "reform movement" begun in Argentina at the University of Córdoba in 1918 was designed not only to popularize and democratize higher education but also to convert the university into a vehicle for effecting fundamental changes in Latin American society.

The potential for intellectual-student political action has been demonstrated on numerous occasions, particularly in the overthrow of traditional *caudillos*. Both intellectuals and students, however, have revealed weaknesses and limitations in their capacity for a leadership role. Some have lent themselves to the exhortations of demagogues and extremists, particularly those of the radical Left. Others have frequently exhibited a lack of originality in adapting foreign philosophies and institutions to the Latin American reality. Thus, the theories they expound often become the subject of argumentative debate rather than a basis for concrete action. Many of their number have succumbed to the influences of a negative nationalism and xenophobia. Others cling to the cult of *arielismo* despite its irrelevance to the area's concrete needs. The freedom allowed university students seems to encourage—if judged by North American standards—a lack of discipline and responsibility which borders on a form of "student anarchy."

While Latin America's diversity permits few generalized judgments concerning the leadership prospects of the intellectual-student tandem, the potential of this group is significant, particularly because it can perform a key function in absorbing and retransmitting the impulses of modernization emanating from the North Atlantic area. The political forces which succeed in harnessing the potential of the intellectual and student will possess an important ally for effecting change and building a greater sense of national cohesion.

Labor

The growth of organized labor in Latin America during the past three decades has made the Latin American worker more aware of the social and economic problems of his nation and of his own potential for influencing the manner in which they are resolved. By the early 1960s, organized labor could claim over twelve million members in Latin America. The value of its support has been recognized by astute politicians, whether they be interested in gaining or maintaining political power, since the general strike can be employed effectively as a political weapon.

Despite its growing sense of power, labor's capacity to exercise a leadership role in Latin American society is at present insignificant. Though in some countries it can be an important political ally, labor's ability to serve as an integrative force on a national scale is minimal. Labor's freedom of action is often severely inhibited by governmental restrictions as well as its own proclivity to promote its interests in the political arena rather than at the collective-bargaining table. Inadequate finances have also led to a crippling dependence upon governmental support. Communist penetration of some labor unions has had the effect of dividing the labor movement. Even the democratic labor groups have failed to achieve real unity. The inter-American labor organization, ORIT, dominates the labor scene, but is faced not only with Communist opposition but also with the competitive efforts of the Christian Democratic trade unions. Attempts to organize agricultural workers have collided with the *patrón-peón* tradition. Hence, organized labor has generally been unable to make itself felt in the rural areas of Latin America.

Many of the above weaknesses of organized labor in Latin America are being attacked by training programs designed to raise the caliber of Latin American union leaders and free the

labor movement from governmental or political party dependence. It is unlikely, however, that the strength of Latin American
labor will grow sufficiently in the foreseeable future to enable it
to assume a major leadership role in the modernization of Latin
American society.

Political Parties

The prospect that organized political parties might provide
dynamic leadership to stimulate change and achieve greater national cohesion is not promising in the light of Latin America's
history. The complex makeup of Latin American political parties
defies brief summarization, and fuller treatment is beyond the
scope of the overview of Latin America's power structure contained in these pages. Nevertheless, even a brief examination of
the region's political party organizations provides the insight
necessary to support a few valid and relevant observations.

Most political parties in Latin America—because of their
personalist bent, extreme opportunism, organizational weaknesses, or other difficulties—have contributed more often to social fragmentation than to national cohesion. There are some
exceptions to this broad generalization, such as the Mexican
Partido Revolucionario Institucional (PRI). The Aprista movement of Peru appeared at one time to offer, like the PRI, another
exception, but this prospect now appears less likely. There
are hopes that the Christian Democratic movement—particularly
its Chilean and Venezuelan branches—might develop the ideological content and integrative force to qualify as an important
factor in creating national cohesion. These hopes, however, remain "on trial" as of the mid-1960s. In short, there are few
political parties in Latin America which possess the ideological
drive or broad popular base which would enable them to exercise an integrative function on a truly national scale.

New Social Sectors

Quite obviously the traditional upper class of Latin America—
frequently labeled as the "oligarchy" or "establishment"—has

demonstrated its inability to provide leadership for effecting dynamic change and building national cohesion. Thus, hopes have been entertained that new and enlightened upper groups as well as the emerging middle sectors might furnish leadership capable of effecting constructive change and building more cohesive societies.

The new and more enlightened upper groups—composed largely of self-made men successful in business, politics, or other professions—suggest an image of self-reliance, dynamism, receptivity to new ideas, and a desire for change. Some members of this important sector conform to such an image. Unfortunately, the lack of homogeneity within the new upper groups impedes their ability to exercise leadership *as a group*, although it is clear that many individual members of this social sector possess leadership capabilities.

The Latin American middle sectors are even more heterogeneous than the new upper groups. A few generalizations concerning their attitudes are possible. The middle sectors are overwhelmingly urban, above average in education, and in favor of industrialization. They support the development of political parties and are frequently nationalistic. Large segments of the Latin American middle sectors that have emerged since the opening of the twentieth century are products of the growth of governmental bureaucracies, the expansion of business and service organizations, and the rapid advance—particularly after 1930—of Latin America's industrialization. Rather than having attained their status as a result of their own efforts, many among the middle sectors have been "made" as a result of a modernization process, the stimulus for which came largely from abroad. Thus, the new social status they acquired "came" more than it was "sought." [11] Salvador de Madariaga, in an incisive comment

[11] For an interesting comparison of the middle sectors in Argentina and Chile with those of Brazil and Mexico, see Bert F. Hoselitz, "El Desarrollo Económico en América Latina," *Desarrollo Económico*, Instituto de Desarrollo Económico y Social, Buenos Aires, Octobre–Diciembre 1962, pp. 49–66. The author notes a dynamism in the middle sectors of the latter two countries which is not characteristic of the former two countries and develops a hypothesis which explains the difference in terms of the *manner* in which these sectors came into being.

on the Latin American middle sectors, says: "There is too much of the idle, unproductive, or merely administrative kind of middle class; not enough, and to a disastrous degree, of the truly productive and creative kind." [12]

Thus, while there are important elements within both the new upper groups and the emerging middle sector of Latin America that offer promise of enlightened leadership, their exercise of such a role cannot be carried out under the banner of the social sector from which they came. In other words, leadership will not be exercised through the medium of these social classes, which are incapable of achieving a clear consensus as to either ends or means. As a result, potential leaders must exert their influence through other channels.

Business Entrepreneurs and Other Professional Groups

Many of the most able leaders to be found in Latin America are members of business and other professional groups. Increasing numbers of these individuals associate themselves with the values of the modern West. As is the case with other Latin American social segments the entrepreneurial and professional groups lack cohesion and a common point of view. The tradition of high-cost and low-unit production for a narrow market endures. Latin American businessmen have among their numbers proponents of economic nationalism who welcome state subsidies or other forms of protection against foreign competition. Many observers have cautioned against equating the dynamic North American entrepreneur with the many Latin American businessmen who cling to deep-rooted Iberian traditions. Such equation frequently leads to the erroneous conclusion that hostility to United States business interests is based on an ideology of state socialism rather than simply the action of competition-shy Latin American "entrepreneurs" who are long accustomed to governmental regulations and protectionism. Consequently, loose identification of the Latin American businessmen's motives and methods with

[12] Salvador de Madariaga, *Latin America between the Eagle and the Bear,* Frederick A. Praeger, Inc., New York, 1962, p. 5.

with those of the North American entrepreneur may do little to convince Latin Americans of the merits of a free economy. Many members of the entrepreneurial group have exhibited little interest in disturbing the rural *status quo*, since they are frequently connected by investment interests, marriage, or family ties with the *latifundista*.

Fortunately, there are a growing number of exceptions to the static and tradition-bound elements within Latin American entrepreneurial and professional groups. In fact, Latin America will depend to a great degree upon the most enlightened individuals among its entrepreneurial and professional groups to give impetus to the region's development.

The New Elite

Latin American development—to the degree that it is a product of the will for dynamic change and spirit of national cohesion—depends upon the emergence of a group that might be termed the "new elite," which includes elements of but is not coincident with any of the institutional, social, or political segments discussed to this point.

The new elite in Latin America is composed of individuals who have adopted the values of the modern West. Its members are intelligent men of vision who are willing to work for constructive change to speed Latin America's modernization. They are prepared to place national interests above narrow group concerns. The new elite is composed of selected churchmen, military leaders, intellectuals and students, labor leaders, businessmen, and a variety of professionals whose proportionate weight and representation will vary from area to area within Latin America. They are members of the new elite not by virtue of their institutional association, social status, or party membership but rather *because of their enlightened attitudes and capactiy for leadership*. Unfortunately—and this is the crux of Latin America's leadership problem—the new elite remains diffused and has yet to create a sufficient number of associations capable of exercising effective direction of their nations' affairs. The creation of such associations is essentially the function of *political action*, and represents the key to Latin America's leadership problem. A Strategy for the Americas must have as a principal objective the identification and support of the new elite, for it represents the principal forces for modernization in Latin America.

5

Contemporary

Currents

The strategist, if he is effectively to formulate policy, must have an anticipatory sense which will enable him to plan for contingencies and establish priorities for action. He must identify and measure the major currents—political, social, and economic—which are shaping Latin America's future. This requirement forces the strategist to generalize about an area of great diversity. As difficult as is this undertaking, it is nonetheless necessary. It is the purpose of this chapter to suggest some of the principal prevailing currents which are relevant to charting the course of United States strategy.

Political Currents

Latin American political parties have gained in strength and maturity. The function of a loyal opposition is better understood than was the case even a generation ago. Popular participation is beginning to restrain the force of *personalismo*, and responsiveness to the popular will and electoral process is growing. Yet democracy in many areas of Latin America remains a goal rather than a reality. Although the traditional *caudillo* is disappearing, periodic reversion to the *golpe de estado* can be expected to be a continuing feature of Latin American politics. All *golpes* do not necessarily represent backward steps. Some *golpista* movements enjoy popular support, and are motivated by constructive ends. It is perhaps indicative of the Latin American political temper that the modern *golpista* frequently justifies his action on the grounds of "preserving constitutional principles" and is usually quick to profess dedication to democratic ideals.

Jacobinismo is the term which perhaps best fits another trend in Latin America. It is motivated more by discontent with a retarded process of modernization than by any coherent political ideology. The *jacobinista* is a political radical, frequently a xenophobe and an advocate of violent social revolution, and sometimes contemptuous of democratic political processes. Some *jacobinistas* describe themselves as Marxists of one variety or another, while others are more ideologically linked with the extreme right. The force of *jacobinismo* in Latin America is on the rise and can be expected to produce revolutionary movements in countries incapable of providing the dynamic leadership needed to effect changes within the limits of evolutionary democratic processes.

Another significant political current in contemporary Latin America is the growth in the structure and the functions of government. Increased state initiative in the economic sphere reflects an impatience with an unsatisfactory rate of economic growth as well as a belief that solutions can be found in more extensive programs of state action. As a result, governmental bureaucracies have steadily expanded. This important trend is rooted less in an ideology of state socialism than in the Iberian tradition of looking to the government for the solution of major problems.

Latin American nationalism will undoubtedly continue to carry both a positive and negative charge and provide the rationale for diverse and at times conflicting objectives. Nationalism, while at times serving as an integrative political ideology, provides the political demagogue with the emotional stimulus for xenophobia and other negative forces. Harnessing the potential of nationalism for constructive ends represents a major challenge to the responsible Latin American politician.

The quest for broader political and economic integration within Latin America represents still another major contemporary current. The prospects for re-creating a Central American confederation have brightened in recent years. Elsewhere in Latin America, however, environmental differences and disparate rates of progress have combined over the course of time with other factors to magnify the differences between individual nations. Nevertheless, a desire for greater Latin American regional unity lingers on. This has been described as a feeling of "emotional commonwealth" or "continental nationalism" and is sometimes expressed in terms of *patria grande* and *latinoamericanismo*. But this sentiment has seldom become more than an intellectual conception and confronts a formidable obstacle, namely, Latin America's diversity. (Yet the problems of Latin American regional unity are certainly fewer than is the case in Africa and Asia.) It is probable that the advocates of *latinoamericanismo*, in the economic as well as political field, will use the forums of the Organization of American States to advance their aims. In other words, the reorganization of OAS administrative machinery may be the vehicle employed to integrate more closely Latin American policies and improve the region's bargaining position with the United States. But the prospects of full political unification in Latin America, i.e., the formation of a real *patria grande*, do not appear bright.

Despite the languid progress made by the Latin American Free Trade Association (LAFTA) organization, an even more ambitious proposal for Latin American integration was initiated by President Eduardo Frei of Chile in January 1965. In response to this overture a group of leading Latin American economists (Raúl Prebisch, Felipe Herrera, José Antonio Mayobre, and Carlos Sanz de Santamaría) advanced in April 1965 a plan calling for a Latin American common market modeled generally after the European Common Market. The plan calls for gradual elimination of tariff barriers between the Latin American nations over a ten-year period, creation of a common tariff system to be applied to nonregional nations, eventual creation of a common currency, regional control over investments in key industrial sectors, organization of joint economic ventures and export enterprises, and free movement of capital and labor within the region. There is little in Latin America's history and environment, however, to suggest the feasibility of such ambitious proposals. A preliminary discussion of the common market plan during the 11th Session of the UN Economic Commission for Latin America, held in Mexico late in May 1965, would indicate that the surrender of national sovereignty required to implement these proposals will find little support among the Latin American nations. Once again, the emotional appeal of *latinoamericanismo* is likely to give way to the hard realities of Latin American diversity. Unfortunately, Latin America's frustrations in its quest of regional integration may well be converted into a sterile effort to use the integration scheme as a bargaining weapon to extract economic concessions from the United States.

Can Pan-Americanism and Latin Americanism coexist? This poses a question of great importance which is periodically reopened but never resolved. Clearly, they are not mutually exclusive concepts although there is a latent antagonism between them which only occasionally comes to the surface. Political and economic realities continue to sustain the idea of hemispheric solidarity expressed by the term "Pan-Americanism." The protective shield of United States military power and reliance on United States markets and economic assistance are practical benefits which Latin Americans are unlikely to overlook. In addition, the OAS has appealed to some in Latin America as a mechanism for blocking unilateral United States action and directing United States power into multilateral channels. Even if the persistent, although nebulous, force of Latin Americanism achieves concrete political form, it is unlikely to displace Pan-Americanism and would probably simply give Pan-Americanism a bilateral rather than multilateral character.

In reality, the contemporary technological revolution—and especially the spectacular achievements of the space age—has rendered obsolete regional concepts confined exclusively to the Western Hemisphere. The forging of closer links between Europe, Latin America, and North America suggests that a triangular relationship—an Atlantic Community of the West—is the political trend of greatest importance to a Strategy for the Americas.[1]

Social Currents

The formation of more complex social structures—the emergence of new upper groups, middle sectors, and an urban proletariat—marks a major social trend in contemporary Latin

[1] This thesis has been developed in chap. 2.

America. The significance of this social flux is obscured by the lack of adequate statistical and analytical studies. Some observations, however, are possible.

Both the new upper groups and the middle sectors are found in highest proportion in the urban areas of Argentina, Chile, Mexico, Uruguay, and Brazil. Here they provide some of the more creative leadership. The paucity of data makes impossible accurate estimates of their quantitative strength and estimates of the degree to which changes in status have produced a transformation in basic cultural values. The social flux occurring in Latin America may broaden the base upon which greater national cohesion can be built, but the heterogeneous attitudes found among both the new upper groups and the middle sectors (as noted in the preceding chapter) make generalizations hazardous about the implications of this social trend.

The expanding urban proletariat in Latin America is also heterogeneous. Some proletarian elements, only a step removed from backward rural areas where the traditional *patrón-peón* relationship has persisted, have displayed little vigor or capacity to contribute to Latin America's growth. Patronal allegiances have frequently been transferred to the demagogue who promises elaborate social welfare benefits or to the government which offers paternalistic blandishments. But a more sophisticated urban proletariat is gradually forming. It possesses greater skills and aspirations as well as some awareness of the illusory nature of social benefits when, as happens so frequently, these are neutralized by rampant inflation. This more knowledgeable section of the urban proletariat has begun to bolster the strength of organized labor in Latin America.

Immigration into Latin America has been of decreasing importance in recent decades. From 1952 through July of 1957, over 1,150,000 immigrants entered Latin America. They have come in greatest numbers from Spain, Italy, and Portugal. Venezuela, Brazil, and Argentina—in that order—were the principal receiving countries.[2] It is unlikely that immigration to Latin America will ever again approach the high tide recorded during the period

[2] Anthony T. Bouscaren, *International Migration since 1945*, Frederick A. Praeger, Inc., New York, 1963, p. 149; and *Migration News*, July–August 1959, p. 30.

1885–1915. Internal migration within Latin America now provides industrial centers with an ample supply of unskilled labor. While Latin America needs and continues to receive some skilled immigrants, the majority in this category have been attracted to other world areas.

An *emigration* of highly skilled individuals from Latin America has taken place in recent years. While this movement appears insignificant in absolute numbers, its high-quality composition (engineers, economists, medical technicians, etc.) represents a serious loss to Latin America.[3] This drain of trained personnel is not offset by present immigration.

Rapid urbanization is a dramatic and highly important development in contemporary Latin America: 46 per cent of the population lives in cities, with 25 per cent concentrated in ten metropolitan areas. The rate of urbanization in Argentina is 67 per cent and is only slightly less in Chile; in Venezuela the rate is 60 per cent and in Colombia 48 per cent. About 40 per cent of the population of Uruguay lives in the capital city of Montevideo. During the next fifteen years, it is estimated that Latin America's cities will increase by an annual average of 4 to 5 per cent. In short, "the character of Latin American nations is becoming an urban one, as already populous cities grow at a dizzying pace."[4]

Latin America's population explosion is also of great social significance. Population has more than doubled between 1920 and 1956 and is expected to reach approximately 600 million by the year 2000. This tremendous growth, coming before the establishment of a modern economy, poses a major impediment to development. Latin America must experience a high rate of economic growth even to maintain existing living standards. By 1975 Latin America must expand its industrial production by 400 per cent and its agricultural production by 120 per cent to main-

---

[3] The *New York Times* on June 2, 1963, reported an estimate of 10,000 emigrants from Argentina to the United States in 1963, with applicants totaling about 25,000. A significant percentage were professional people, skilled technicians, small businessmen, and newly trained industrial workers.

[4] Charles M. Haar, "Latin America's Troubled Cities," *Foreign Affairs*, April 1963, pp. 539–540.

tain present growth rates. Within the same period, Latin America's labor force will have increased by 35 million even though not more than 5 million new jobs can be expected to develop within the agricultural sector.[5]

Of considerable importance is the high proportion of youth in Latin America's demographic pattern. Approximately 40 per cent of the population is under fifteen years of age.[6] The energy and drive of youth can be expected to accelerate the pace of development. However, if rapid evolutionary changes cannot be effected, youthful impatience may force the modernization process in ways which may not suit advocates of moderation.

Economic Trends

Latin America occupies an intermediate position among world regions as judged by various indices of economic growth and by the complexity of its economic structure. In fact, by such measurements, Latin America ranks closer to the more advanced industrial nations than to the less developed areas of Asia and Africa. During the period 1945–1960, Latin America's gross national product (measured in constant prices) rose at an average annual rate of 4.7 per cent—a record of growth that exceeded that of the United States, Canada, and most countries of Western Europe.[7] However, since 1960, the pace of Latin American economic growth has slackened. The causes for this trend are of considerable importance to a Strategy for the Americas.

One of the main shortcomings of the Latin American economy

[5] United Nations, Department of Economic and Social Affairs, *1963 Report on the World Social Situation*, E/CN. 5/375/Rev. 1, United Nations, Department of Public Information, New York, 1963, p. 123.

[6] United Nations, Department of Economic and Social Affairs, *Demographic Yearbook 1961*, United Nations, Department of Public Information, New York, 1961, pp. 138–159.

[7] Latin American growth figures are from the United Nations, Economic Commission for Latin America (ECLA), *The Economic Development of Latin America in the Post-War Period*, E/CN. 12/659/Add. 1, Mar del Plata, Argentina, United Nations, 1963, vol. 2, p. 20. For comparative purposes, the GNP of the United States increased during the same period at an average annual rate of approximately 2.3 per cent.

is low agricultural productivity.[8] Agriculture in 1945 contributed 25 per cent of the GNP and absorbed 57 per cent of the labor force; by 1960, these percentages had decreased to 21.6 per cent and 47.3 per cent respectively. The shift of rural population to urban areas and the drive for industrialization have formed the two principal responses of Latin America to the relatively low productivity per worker in the agricultural sector.

Many problems have been encountered in translating these changes into increased economic output. The industrial sector has absorbed but a fraction of the labor force which has shifted out of agriculture. A disproportionate share of surplus agricultural labor has moved into the services sector—a broad and diversified segment of Latin America's productive structure. In 1945 the services sector contributed 16.1 per cent of Latin America's GNP and employed 11.4 per cent of the area's work force. By 1960 the services sector's GNP contribution had decreased to 15.7 per cent while its share of the labor force had increased to 15.8 per cent. Productivity of the services sector was thus reduced by the infusion of illiterate and unskilled rural laborers. The inability of the manufacturing-industry sector to absorb a greater proportion of the shifting labor force is explained in part by the low purchasing power of rural areas which restricts the market possibilities for manufactured items. Limited purchasing power in the rural areas, in turn, is explained largely by low agrarian productivity. This vicious circle demonstrates dramatically that Latin America's economy requires a cycle of interdependent rural-urban growth.[9]

Efforts to generate an interdependent cycle of rural-urban growth have concentrated on a many-faceted program bearing the much used but frequently abused term "agrarian reform." Agrarian reform in the popular mind has been frequently equated with revision of Latin America's land-tenure system, i.e.,

[8] In the discussion which follows, output percentage contributions to gross national product are from *ibid.*, p. 21. Sectoral employment percentages are from *ibid.*, p. 26.

[9] For a provocative analysis of the problems and some proposed methods of creating a national market see Walter W. Rostow, *How to Make a National Market* (address before the 17th Annual Convention of the Farm Equipment Institute, New Orleans, Oct. 1, 1963; published as Department of State Press Release No. 498, Oct. 1, 1963).

with the breakup of the *latifundia* and the distribution of their acreage to landless peasants. This is a grossly oversimplified version of the agrarian problem. While the *latifundia* have generally been inefficient producers, land redistribution is not always the simple solution it might appear to be. Some farm and grazing lands can be productively worked only in large parcels. Experience has shown that efficient production requires more than the donation of a parcel of land to the peasant. He will, in most instances, need capital or easy credit for the purchase of seeds, machinery, and fertilizers. He may also require technical advice and marketing assistance.

Agricultural cooperatives have been useful in meeting some of these needs, but the capital necessary to launch such programs must usually be supplied by national governments heavily burdened by other demands. Such practical considerations have given rise to alternative measures which wisely focus on increased productivity rather than land redistribution per se. Tax laws have been enacted to force the *latifundista* to farm efficiently or to sell unproductive portions of his holdings. The problem in most cases is not the *latifundia* as a form of land tenure but rather the *latifundista* mentality which—in the Iberian tradition—often views land as a prestige symbol rather than a basis for vigorous agrarian enterprise.

Even if Latin America's agrarian productivity makes great strides, the marketability of and the income received from its produce remain a major problem. The marketing problem also affects the mining sector. Extreme specialization in agricultural and mineral products, both of which are heavily dependent upon export markets, is a dominant characteristic of the area's economies. From 1954 to 1956, for example, 90 per cent of Latin America's export proceeds came from agricultural and mineral products, with agriculture providing about two-thirds of the total. Projections for the year 1975 indicate that this level of dependence will be decreased only to 85 per cent.[10] The primary-products problem promises to be a continuing one. Venezuela obtains 93 per cent of

[10] The agrarian-mining proportionate contribution will, however, shift in favor of mining. Rather than contributing one-third of the 90 per cent of foreign exchange earned by primary products in 1954–1956, mining will contribute four-tenths of the 85 per cent contributions made by the agri-

its export earnings from petroleum; Guatemala, El Salvador, and Colombia each obtain between 72 and 77 per cent of their export income from coffee. Two principal export products earn the following: Colombia, 92 per cent (coffee and petroleum); Costa Rica, 86 per cent (coffee and bananas); the Dominican Republic, 93 per cent (sugar and tobacco); Guatemala, 89 per cent (coffee and cotton); Haiti, 85 per cent (coffee and bananas).[11]

Latin America's heavy reliance upon the export of primary commodities is precarious in view of the instability of the world market for such products. Fluctuations in the price and sales volume of primary products are caused by the inelastic supply of some commodities, inelastic demand for others, and a combination of both factors in the case of still other products. Falling proceeds from primary product exports force the Latin American nations either to curtail their imports or seek financial assistance to cover an unfavorable balance of payments. This situation gives rise to the Latin American complaint of "adverse terms of trade" which some of the area's economists regard as a long-term phenomenon hostile to Latin America's interests.[12]

Many Latin Americans have urged strongly that their primary-products problem be met by an international commodity agree-

---

culture and mining sectors in 1975. See Victor L. Urquidi, *Viabilidad Económica de América Latina*, Fondo de Cultura Económica, Mexico City, 1962, p. 187; based on ECLA report *El Mercado Común Latinoamericano*, E/CN.12/531, United Nations, Department of Public Information, New York, 1959.

[11] B. Golomb and R. H. Dolkart (eds.), *Statistical Abstract of Latin America 1962*, Center of Latin American Studies, University of California, Los Angeles, 1962, p. 98.

[12] Raúl Prebisch, a well-known Latin American economist, holds to a view that Latin American terms of trade are deteriorating continuously over time on account of the differing nature of the price structure in the developed and underdeveloped world. Prebisch's views are stated in Raúl Prebisch, *The Economic Development of Latin America and Its Principal Problems*, E/CN. 12/89/Rev., United Nations, Department of Public Information, New York, 1950; or Raúl Prebisch, "The Role of Commercial Policies in the Under-developed Countries," *American Economic Review, Papers and Proceedings*, May 1959, pp. 251–273. For a critique of the Prebisch thesis see Gottfried Haberler, "Terms of Trade and Economic Development," in H. C. Ellis (ed.), *Economic Development for Latin America*, St. Martin's Press, Inc., New York, 1961, pp. 275–297.

ment of one form or another. The desirability, feasibility, and effect of such agreements have been a matter of considerable debate. Commodity-stabilization plans—which aim essentially at stabilization of supply and demand of the commodity in question—have been negotiated for such commodities as wheat, sugar, coffee, and tin. The stabilization approach, however, has encountered many difficulties. Price ranges are both difficult to establish and to maintain over long periods; terms are not easily enforced, particularly during abnormal market periods; but, most of all, commodity-stabilization agreements are basically palliatives in a market which is inherently unstable.

Unsatisfactory experience with commodity-stabilization plans has generated increasing interest in the "compensation agreement"—basically a countercyclical loan designed to relieve a crisis in balance of payments caused by a shortfall in export receipts. Countercyclical loans normally are conditional upon the borrower's taking action mutually agreed upon as necessary to repay the debt and to lessen his vulnerability to the recurrence of similar balance-of-payments crises in the future. The compensation agreement would have as its general objective to remove the borrower's economy from excessive dependence upon vulnerable export products by encouraging the building of a more diversified productive structure. The UN and the OAS have advanced compensation proposals, and both the International Monetary Fund and the United States Export-Import Bank have made loans to the Latin American nations which were in fact— even if not in name—basically countercyclical in nature.

Increased agrarian productivity and more stable proceeds from primary-commodity exports will not by themselves solve Latin America's economic problems. Another major weakness is the capital-formation process which determines the level and direction of Latin American investment. Gross investment in Latin America during the postwar era has drawn upon domestic sources for 90 per cent of its capital. While the remaining 10 per cent coming from foreign sources plays a particularly important role, it is nevertheless clear that increases in Latin American investment will depend to an important degree upon *domestic* Latin American capital formation.

During the late 1950s and early 1960s, the share of public

capital in Latin America's domestic investment process has increased. In Argentina, Brazil, Colombia, Chile, Ecuador, Mexico, Peru, and Venezuela the relative contribution of the public sector to domestic capital formation grew from 25 per cent in 1958 to 31 per cent in 1959 and 32 per cent in 1960.[13] This investment has been directed mostly toward infrastructure projects.

A detailed examination of private investment from domestic Latin American sources is hampered by the lack of adequate statistical data. This fact in itself indicates that private investment in Latin America is largely the result of the highly personal decisions of a relatively small high-income group rather than the lending and credit operations of commercial banking institutions, which normally keep extensive records of their financial operations. Despite a dearth of data, it is evident that private entrepreneurs have concentrated their investments heavily in land and in the construction of luxury dwellings. A large proportion of private capital in Latin America tends to be channeled into activities which are relatively unproductive from the point of view of overall national economic growth. Moreover, a considerable portion of private savings have found their way abroad.

The reasons for the lack of a more productive private investment pattern in Latin America are many and diverse: political instability; unsound governmental fiscal and monetary policies, including measures leading to rampant inflation; excessive governmental intervention in the private sector; lack of adequate credit and banking institutions; shortage of technical and administrative talent; and the pervasiveness of traditional Iberian cultural values inhibiting the creation of a dynamic entrepreneurial spirit. The resolution of such complex problems depends, in the final analysis, upon changes in basic values as well as able and courageous political leadership.

It is with this frame of reference that contemporary Latin

[13] Institute of International Studies and Overseas Administration of the University of Oregon, "Problems of Latin American Economic Development," in United States Senate, Subcommittee on American Republics Affairs of the Committee on Foreign Relations, *United States–Latin American Relations*, 86th Cong. 2d Sess., 1960, p. 578.

American arrangements for a common market should be assessed. The Central American Common Market (CACM) has already achieved noteworthy advances; intra-CACM trade tripled during a period of five years. CACM aims at creating a nearly unified market by 1966. CACM's progress must be viewed in perspective: it contains only 5.6 per cent of Latin America's population and produces only 3.7 per cent of Latin America's gross domestic product.[14] The LAFTA has taken a more cautious approach, but it has made headway and is expected to give Latin American economies a much-needed impulse. LAFTA hopes to be the means for expansion of domestic markets and rationalization of industrial development. LAFTA members constitute almost 85 per cent of Latin America's population and produce just over 80 per cent of the region's gross domestic product (which in 1960 totaled $64.5 billion). Substantially free intra-LAFTA trade is planned by 1973, but progress toward this goal has been slow. LAFTA faces enormous obstacles. Intra-LAFTA trade comprises only 10 per cent of its membership's total commerce. Geography impedes overland travel. Given the small volume of intra-LAFTA trade, sea shipments are often expensive. Perhaps the most difficult problem is that major imports simply cannot be supplied from within LAFTA, although alleviation of this handicap is, of course, one of the objectives of the organization.[15]

Latin America's dissatisfaction with its progress in achieving effective economic integration is reflected in the new proposal advanced in April 1965 which would submerge both CACM and LAFTA within a new regional bloc patterned on the European Common Market. The proposal calls for the elimination of internal tariffs within ten years, a common tariff system to be applied to imports from outside the region, control over common investments in key industrial sectors, a common monetary unit and payments union, free movement of capital and labor, and joint export enterprises cutting across national boundaries. This

[14] *Latin American Business Highlights*, Chase Manhattan Bank, First Quarter, 1964, p. 11.
[15] *Ibid.*, pp. 8–11; also *Latin American Business Highlights*, 2d Quarter, 1963, pp. 3–7.

is an ambitious scheme which—whatever its economic merits—appears unlikely to gain either full or rapid acceptance.

Whatever the fate of the Latin American common market proposal, there are limits to the benefits which Latin American economic integration can be expected to yield unless it is accompanied by a more dynamic capital-formation and investment pattern within member countries. It is clear that economic growth, whether measured in terms of GNP or other materialistic criteria, is but one component of the challenge of development. Fundamental human attitudes must be transformed. This is the *real* challenge to Latin Americans, and to an overwhelming degree these changes depend upon *Latin American* efforts. Many economic ailments clearly require decisions which can be taken only by enlightened political leadership.

Relevance of Latin American Reality to United States Strategy

The United States policy maker faces problems in Latin America which defy simple, generalized solutions. United States policies and programs must be tailored to Latin America's environmental and human diversity; they must also be administered with great flexibility. The policy maker, if he is to understand the Latin American reality, must develop a high degree of cultural empathy. Modern Western attitudes have undermined traditional Iberian cultural values. In their place, Latin Americans will develop their own distinctive institutions rather than simply follow foreign models. The United States policy maker must acquire an understanding of this cultural transition, together with patience and tolerance for diversity. He must realize that United States conceptions of political democracy, private enterprise, and social egalitarianism cannot be transferred to Latin America without passing through an Iberian filter that will give them new meaning and application.

A grasp of basic trends and patterns in Latin America would enable the policy maker to formulate the priorities upon which the United States must concentrate its attention: those leverage points most likely to accelerate Latin American development and closer identification with the modern West. The phenomena of rapid urbanization and the concentration of growth within fringe lands suggest geographic priorities for United States policy in Latin America. The population explosion, creating a demographic pattern in which young people are predominant, has important implications for a wide range of United States policy decisions.

The United States must help Latin America develop its human resources through a rapid expansion and improvement in educational facilities, thus increasing Latin American capabilities for absorbing the "New Enlightenment" of the modern West. Latin America's ability to achieve rapid economic growth hinges primarily upon the accomplishment of four tasks: a rise in agrarian productivity; a reduction of the adverse effects of world market instability in primary commodities; a rise in the level and productive employment of domestic private investments; and the encouragement of greater economic integration through common market arrangements.

Latin American efforts to achieve regional integration—such as LAFTA and CACM in the economic sphere—are highly relevant to United States strategic interests. Closer economic and political collaboration among Latin American nations could have either positive or negative implication for the United States, depending upon the spirit by which the advocates of *latinoamericanismo* are moved. Since attempts to achieve more effective Latin American unity face major obstacles, particularly in the political field, the concrete accomplishments and benefits of *panamericanismo* remain a matter of common hemispheric interest. Perhaps the most important insight to be drawn from contemporary trends toward regionalism is that *long-term trends toward closer unity within the Atlantic World are likely to build stronger ties between the more advanced areas of Latin America and the North Atlantic Community than are likely to be created among the Latin American nations themselves.*

An examination of contemporary currents in Latin America yields certain conclusions of relevance to the United States policy maker. On the one hand, evolutionary processes that help to integrate the disparate elements of Latin American society are often more constructive than pressures for rapid social changes which in some instances can be disruptive. On the other hand, where evolutionary progress has been stymied and the process of modernization appears likely to take a revolutionary path, the United States must learn to deal with and attempt to guide these revolutionary forces rather than abandon them to the Communists or other extremist elements. The United States policy maker must attempt to direct the force of Latin American nationalism toward constructive ends rather than leave it for anti-Yankee elements to capture and manipulate.

Constructive and dynamic change within Latin America depends largely upon the efforts of an emerging new elite. Of the many social segments from which the new elite comes, none is capable alone of providing the leadership necessary to achieve national cohesion. It is the new elite, cutting across society, which must assume the formidable task of leadership in Latin America. Political action, it has been suggested, is the key to welding the new elite into an effective force.[16] The policy maker must link United States resources with the leadership capabilities of Latin America's new elite with greater deftness, sophistication, and political realism than has been evident in the past.

[16] See chap. 3 for a discussion of the importance of political action and chap. 4 for an examination of the role of the new elite in the formulation of a Strategy for the Americas.

6

United States—

Latin American

Issues

Several issues have produced a fundamental cleavage between Latin America and its powerful neighbor to the north. On the one hand, many Latin Americans innately fear United States power; others simply envy United States material wealth. On the other hand, the United States chafes at the seeming inability of many Latin Americans to assume greater civic responsibilities and generate the dynamism needed to effect a more rapid modernization of their societies.

Latin American complaints against the United States center upon four issues: neglect, intervention, support of dictatorships, and economic exploitation. The United States, in turn, complains about Latin America's general lack of understanding of United States worldwide commitments; the failure of some Latin Americans to grasp fully the danger of Communist subversion and to meet treaty commitments calling for collective action against extrahemispheric intervention; and the ambivalence of many Latin Americans when the nonintervention principle—as they conceive it—conflicts with their professed support for popular sovereignty and representative democracy.

In charging the United States with "neglect," Latin Americans most frequently refer to Marshall Plan aid to Western Europe and United States military assistance to such countries as Greece, Turkey, and Nationalist China immediately following World War II. While areas outside the Western Hemisphere did receive the largest share of United States attention and assistance during the decade following World War II, the United States objective was to speed the recovery of war-torn allies and defend countries menaced by Communist expansion. However, Latin America profited indirectly from the Marshall Plan. The recovery of European economies resulted in increased markets for Latin American primary products and a renewed contribution of European capital to Latin American economic development. United States military and economic aid to countries in the Eastern Mediterranean and Asia strengthened the defense of the West in general—an objective which most Latin Americans would agree is inseparable from their own interests.

An increasingly strong current of Latin American opinion, however, does not acknowledge a full identity of interest between the nations of Latin America and the North Atlantic area on all cold war issues. Some of these issues seem remote to Latin Americans confronted by the seemingly more immediate tasks of socioeconomic development. Many Latin Americans do not recognize the relationship between United States extrahemispheric commitments and United States efforts to help them solve their own socioeconomic problems. Rarely do they perceive that United States contributions to Latin American development could be enormously increased if the unwelcome burdens of the cold war could be removed. However, such a conversion of resources must await the abandonment of Communist expansionist policies, subversive tactics, and opposition to effective arms-control measures.

The United States defense against the charge of neglect is not convincing to Latin Americans who recall that, during the sixteen-year period from July 1, 1945, to June 30, 1961, no Latin American nation received as much United States governmental aid as Tito's Yugoslavia. During the same period, the financial aid extended to Yugoslavia and Poland amounted to more than 50 per cent of that granted to all countries in Latin America.[1] Similarly, United States refusal to establish an inter-American bank during the mid-1950s—an attitude later reversed after con-

[1] United States Agency for International Development, *U. S. Foreign Assistance and Assistance from International Organizations, July 1, 1945–June 30, 1961,* rev. ed., 1962, pp. 2, 3, 25, 62.

siderable Latin American pressure—and the traditionally negative United States reaction to commodity-stabilization plans
advocated by Latin American nations were interpreted as examples of United States neglect.

The Latin American charge of neglect has not been confined
to material matters alone. The United States has been criticized
for allegedly lacking a "human comprehension of what was
going on in the hearts and minds of millions of Latin American
neighbors," [2] as well as for failing on many occasions to consult
Latin American heads of state, or even keep them informed, on
issues of the East-West conflict which affect the West in general.
Another complaint among Latin Americans is that United States
newspapers are crisis-oriented in their Latin American coverage.
Few United States news media—largely because of public dis-
interest—have systematically reported Latin American events.
On the matter of tourism, areas beyond Mexico, Central America, and the Caribbean islands feel slighted. In recent years,
only about 3 to 4 per cent of the total expenditures made by
North American tourists abroad have been made in South America.

Americans north of the Rio Grande, however, are entitled to
reply to such charges. They might well ask where in Latin
America is there an effort comparable to that being made today
by many North American universities, institutes, and foundations
to reach a better understanding of the Latin American conditions? The Latin American press has also been sensation-oriented
in its coverage of United States events. The frequent inclination
to consider the cold war as a "United States problem" smacks of
neglect on the part of Latin America.

Perhaps these charges and countercharges of neglect can best
be met with a candid comment: Inter-American conferences
filled with flowery prose about common ideals and interests all
too often simply mask the mutual predilection of North Americans and Latin Americans alike for crisis diplomacy and pursuit
of narrow self-interest.

Without question, no United States–Latin American issue is

[2] John C. Dreier, *The Organization of American States and the Hemispheric
Crisis*, Harper & Row, Publishers, Incorporated, for the Council on Foreign
Relations, New York, 1962, pp. 3–4.

subject to more debate, emotional reaction, and conflict of principle than that of intervention. This issue is almost always couched in terms of United States meddling in Latin American affairs. The charge is evoked most often by Latin American memories of United States conduct in the Caribbean area during the years 1900–1930, when the United States intervened in Cuba, Panama, Nicaragua, Honduras, Mexico, the Dominican Republic, and Haiti. United States actions were explained, whether justified or not, by many circumstances: severe provocation of one kind or another, a desire to prevent European intervention, and a need to protect the lives and property of United States citizens under conditions approaching anarchy. United States interventions were short in duration and took no advantage of opportunities for territorial aggrandizement. If the United States indeed succumbed to imperialistic urges, the essential nature of the tendency was one of restraint. The mood has been termed appropriately as "imperialism with an uneasy conscience." [3] None of these explanations satisfied Latin American critics. Intellectuals led by Darío of Nicaragua, Rodó of Uruguay, and Ugarte of Argentina voiced sharp criticism and evoked widespread support for their views.

This thirty-year period of sporadic United States intervention impeded constructive growth of the inter-American system. The legacy was "permanent scars." [4] An important but regrettable byproduct was the evolution of "absolute nonintervention"—a concept unsuccessfully urged upon the United States by Latin American nations during the Pan-American Conference of 1928 in Havana and finally accepted without reservation by the United States at the Buenos Aires Conference of 1936. The concept of absolute nonintervention, eventually incorporated in the Charter of the Organization of American States (Articles 15, 16, and 17) drafted in 1948 at Bogotá remains a firm precept of the inter-American system. [5]

[3] Dexter Perkins, *Hands Off: A History of the Monroe Doctrine*, Little, Brown and Company, Boston, 1941, p. 230.

[4] Dreier, *op. cit.*, p. 19; Samuel Flagg Bemis, *The Latin American Policy of the United States*, Harcourt, Brace & World, Inc., New York, 1943, p. 157.

[5] Article 15: No State or group of States has the right to intervene, directly or indirectly, for any reason whatever, in the internal or external affairs of

Unfortunately, the "finality" with which Pan-American conferences and the OAS Charter have treated the issue of intervention has not dispelled the aura of unreality which surrounds this concept in its absolute form. The United States can be accused of "intervention" whether it acts or not. Refusal to exercise power may, in effect, abandon a people to tyranny and betray the principle of popular sovereignty to which the nations of the Americas have repeatedly pledged adherence. The fact that power can be exercised for noble and moral purposes is frequently ignored in the emotional atmosphere generated by the issue of "Yankee intervention." In many cases of alleged intervention a *moral* judgment is involved although this facet is frequently not recognized. Nonintervention will not work as a unilateral rule applied by the United States but unaccepted by other governments. As John Stuart Mill observed:

> The doctrine of non-intervention, to be a legitimate principle of morality, must be accepted by all governments. The despots must consent to be bound by it as well as the free States. Unless they do, the profession of it by free countries comes to but this miserable issue, that the wrong side may help the wrong, but the right must not help the right.[6]

Never has an inter-American conference arrived at an acceptable definition of intervention. Consequently, the solemn dis-

---

any other State. The foregoing principle prohibits not only armed force but also any other form of interference or attempted threat against the personality of the State or against its political, economic and cultural elements.

Article 16: No State may use or encourage the use of coercive measures of an economic or political character in order to force the sovereign will of another State and obtain from it advantages of any kind.

Article 17: The territory of a State is inviolable; it may not be the object, even temporarily, of military occupation or of other measures of force taken by another State, directly or indirectly, on any grounds whatever. No territorial acquisitions or special advantages obtained either by force or by other means of coercion shall be recognized.

Charter of the Organization of American States, 341. 1-E-4667, Treaty Series I, Pan American Union, Washington, D.C., 1957, pp. 4–5.

[6] John Stuart Mill, "A Few Words on Non-Intervention," *Dissertations and Discussions: Political, Philosophical and Historical*, 2d ed., London, 1875, vol. III, p. 176.

avowal of an undefined concept of intervention leaves open to interpretation the limits of this commitment. To assert the concept in sweeping terms and to defend it stubbornly does nothing to dispel the fog. In a world of sovereign nation-states and in the absence of world law, what is "intervention" to one nation may be "defense of national interests" to another. The Pan-American conferees who agreed at Buenos Aires in 1936 to an unqualified and undefined concept of intervention were no doubt influenced by the history of United States intervention in the Caribbean in preceding decades. They sought to proscribe such actions as the landing of marines and seizure of customs revenues, but they could not be expected to foresee in 1936 the conflict techniques of Communist tacticians, who not only circumvent but also misconstrue the nonintervention precept in order to sow dissension among the nations of the Americas, as well as to thwart an effective Western response to Communist infiltration.

Inter-American conferences have since recognized the threat of communism and its use of the nonintervention concept as a divisive weapon. Condemning the unilateral use of power by any one American nation, OAS representatives have concentrated upon devising an acceptable formula for *multilateral* action. The Rio Defense Treaty of 1947, the basic instrument for defense of the Western Hemisphere, provides only for consultations "to agree on measures to be taken" in response to aggression from sources outside the hemisphere. Realizing the need for stronger defenses against Communist infiltration, the Caracas Conference of 1954 passed a resolution which stated that:

> The domination or control of the political institutions of any American State by the international Communist movement, extending to this Hemisphere the political system of an extra-continental power, would constitute a threat to the sovereignty and political independence of the American States, endangering the peace of America, and would call for a Meeting of Consultation to consider the adoption of appropriate action in accordance with existing treaties.[7]

[7] *Tenth Inter-American Conference: Final Act,* 341. 1-E-5218, Pan American Union, Washington, D.C., 1954, pp. 94–95.

Unfortunately, when the time arrives to consider the adoption of appropriate action, the difference between the United States and Latin American assessments of the Communist danger becomes apparent. Stripped of its legalistic hedging, Latin American recalcitrance toward supporting effective collective action against Communist subversion is based not only on a differing assessment of the threat but also upon a basic distrust of the United States. There is a widespread feeling that the Communist issue may be used as a screen for Yankee intervention. Stated bluntly, some Latin Americans fear United States intervention more than Communist infiltration and subversion.

The Cuban episode put inter-American resolutions to resist extrahemispheric intervention to a signal test. The confrontation between the United States and the Soviet Union during the Cuban missile crisis of October 1962 finally rallied unanimous Latin American support for appropriate action. Even this support was qualified, since direct United States military action against Cuba was expressly exempted by the OAS interpretation of appropriate action.

United States intervention during the Dominican Republic crisis of April–June 1965 has once again opened the United States to widespread criticism for taking unilateral action in violation of Article 15 of the OAS Charter. The United States contention that immediate action was required to protect the lives of United States and other foreign nationals and to prevent the revolution from falling under the control of Communists will probably long remain a matter of debate. History, as Lord Acton pointed out, does not disclose its alternatives. It is beyond debate, however, that the OAS was unprepared—even if it were so disposed—to influence the course of events during this crisis. Clearly, what is needed is a strengthening of the OAS peace-keeping machinery to include a multilateral inter-American force capable of rapid deployment to give practical effect to the Caracas Resolution of 1954, cited previously, as well as to support other principles which the OAS upholds. Perhaps most difficult of all, there must be greater agreement between OAS members as to what constitutes appropriate action in emergency situations which permit a minimum time for consultation and no time for ineffectual debate such as initially characterized the OAS handling of the Dominican crisis. In short, Article 15 of the OAS Charter must be reconciled with contemporary world realities.

The concept of nonintervention must be reconciled with other cherished inter-American principles such as human rights, popular sovereignty, and self-determination. Belief in the self-determination of peoples is, after all, the foundation upon which the concept of nonintervention rests. Yet when a Latin American government suppresses the basic freedoms of its own population, a conflict arises between defense of human rights and adherence to an absolute concept of nonintervention. Perhaps the clearest defense of human rights when they conflict with the concept of nonintervention was made by Eduardo Rodríguez Larreta, a former Uruguayan Foreign Minister. In November 1945, he stated in a note addressed to all member nations of the Pan American Union that:

> The principle of non-intervention by one State in the affairs of another, in the field of inter-American relations, constitutes in itself a great advance. . . . It must, however, be harmonized with other principles, . . . the minimum human liberties within a civilized continent—wherever they are notoriously and persistently infringed or ignored. . . . Therefore a multilateral collective action, exercised with complete unselfishness of all the other republics of the continent, aimed at achieving in a spirit of brotherly prudence the mere re-establishment of essential rights, and directed toward the fulfillment of freely contracted juridical obligations, must not be held to injure the government affected, but rather it must be recognized as being taken for the benefit of all, including the country which has been suffering under such a harsh regime.[8]

The United States quickly endorsed the Larreta position in a statement which declared:

> If they are to preserve the peace, the American republics cannot permit oppressive regimes to exist in their midst, because such regimes, prompted by the instinct of self-preservation in an environment hostile to them, must spread out in order to survive. . . . Violation of the elementary rights of man by a government

[8] *Department of State Bulletin*, Nov. 25, 1945, pp. 865–866.

of force and the non-fulfillment of obligations by such a government is a matter of common concern to all the republics. As such, it justifies collective multilateral action after full consultation among the republics in accordance with established procedures.[9]

The Rodríguez Larreta proposal was not adopted. It was defeated by the same force which has frustrated more effective hemispheric defense against Communist infiltration: a deeply rooted Latin American distrust of the United States. It is with reference to this fear that a Mexican Foreign Office official stated:

> Latin America has been hindered from carrying out formulas which would mean democratic progress and a higher level of coexistence in America. While this fear exists, while the present situation does not change, the cornerstone of the inter-American system, its guiding principle, will not be democracy, but intransigent non-intervention. . . . Other principles, excellent in themselves, like the international protection of democracy and human rights and the non-recognition of dictatorships imposed by violence, have not been established in America for fear that they might be used as instruments of intervention in the Latin American countries.[10]

The conflict between the concept of absolute non-intervention and democratic ideals troubles many Latin American thinkers. Antonio Gómez Robledo, a distinguished Mexican jurist, expressed the view of many in questioning the primacy of nonintervention when it conflicted with human rights and representative democracy.[11] Gonzalo J. Facio, President of the OAS Council, supported early in 1963 the earlier views of Rodríguez Larreta and Gómez Robledo.[12] Thus, the view that nonintervention must be reconciled with other important principles continues to command attention within the Americas.

Dictatorial regimes which exercise power contrary to the pop-

---

[9] *Ibid.*, Dec. 2, 1945, p. 892.

[10] Jorge Castañeda, "Pan Americanism and Regionalism: A Mexican View," *International Organization*, August 1956, pp. 385, 387.

[11] Antonio Gómez Robledo, *Idea y Experiencia de América,* Fondo de Cultura Económica, Mexico City, 1958, p. 239.

[12] Gonzalo J. Facio, "Los Golpes de Estado y la No Intervención," *Panoramas,* Enero–Febrero 1963, pp. 5–58.

ular will pose another dilemma to United States policy makers. Should such regimes be recognized and admitted into the OAS? If recognition is granted, should economic or military assistance be extended? Should recognition and support be conditioned on a firm commitment to permit free elections? [13] The issues of dictatorship, recognition, and nonintervention are closely related. United States hesitation in granting diplomatic recognition has been interpreted in some instances as intervention, even when a legitimate government has been ousted by a military *junta*. Yet, ironically, the United States has borne the brunt of criticism for its alleged support of authoritarian regimes.

Charges of United States support of dictatorial Latin American regimes were most vociferous during the 1950s. The United States position was compromised by a policy of expediency prompted largely by circumstances of the cold war. Facing Soviet expansionism, United States aims in Latin America were reduced to maintenance of peace, defense of strategic areas, and continued access to vital raw materials. United States leaders believed that the global situation necessitated stable hemispheric governments of anti-Communist conviction.

If the United States has handled awkwardly its relationships with dictatorial Latin American governments and is thereby vulnerable to just criticism, some Latin American nations are equally vulnerable to the same charge. Latin American obsession with nonintervention has impeded the type of multilateral action which Rodríguez Larreta proposed in defense of human rights and popular sovereignty. Castro came to power with the promise of reestablishing the democratic Cuban constitution of 1940 and granting the Cuban people the privilege of choosing their government by free elections. Instead, Castro imposed tyranny on the Cuban people. Yet many Latin American leaders were slow to condemn the Communist dictatorship of Castro's

---

[13] *Ibid.* Facio, basing much of his discussion on Rodríguez Larreta's proposal, develops fully the question of recognition, arguing that recognition should be withheld from regimes which deny the exercise of popular sovereignty. Clearly implicit in his argument is the primacy of popular sovereignty over the concept of nonintervention when a conflict arises in connection with the granting or withholding of diplomatic recognition.

Cuba and have been slower still to support concrete measures to combat Castro-inspired subversion, much less work actively for the liberation of the Cuban people.

Still another charge leveled against the United States by some Latin Americans is that of "economic exploitation." A historical basis exists for such an allegation in the operations of some United States business enterprises during the early decades of the century and in governmental policies during the eras of the Big Stick and Dollar Diplomacy. The charge of economic exploitation in recent years has taken on an essentially psychological aspect. The sheer weight of United States economic power causes an adverse psychological reaction among Latin Americans, particularly when foreign interests control large segments of a given Latin American economy.

Statistics reveal the economic power wielded by some of the larger United States corporations. For example, petroleum taxes formed 57 per cent of Venezuela's revenues; in 1955 approximately one-half of these revenues were collected from one United States firm, Creole Petroleum Corporation. The governmental revenues of Costa Rica, Panama, and Honduras totaled $121 million in 1955, while the consolidated statement of the United Fruit Company for that year showed a gross revenue of $330 million.

While the large-scale operations of these and other United States firms in Latin America offer many benefits—some of which will be discussed in Chapter 8—their massiveness overawes. This observation should not be at all surprising, since private United States economic power also causes concern in more developed areas such as Canada and some countries of Western Europe. The United States government, in taking actions designed to protect the legitimate interests of United States firms, must tread warily in order to avoid aggravating problems which are frequently emotion-packed and ready-made for anti-Yankee exploitation. Delineation of the line dividing economic "neglect" from "exploitation" in United States–Latin American relations is a problem that clearly transcends economics.

Many of the barriers to harmonization of inter-American interests and relations are basically *psychological*. The sheer weight of United States power and material wealth has produced adverse psychological reactions. The very process of modernization which Latin America is experiencing has generated tensions which frequently are manifested in extreme nationalism and xenophobia. There are some real and tangible conflicts of interests between the Americas which pose obstacles to cordial inter-American relations, but most of the problems would lend themselves to ready solution if the atmosphere within which they are considered could be improved. One of the major difficulties in achieving a better atmosphere is posed by the adroit exploitation of United States–Latin American issues by Communist tacticians. It is to this subject that we now turn.

7

Communism

in the

Americas

Communism poses the major external threat to peace, harmony, and orderly progress within the Americas. Soviet grand strategy aims to prevent closer integration of the North Atlantic Community and block greater identification of Latin America with the Western world. The Soviet Union is motivated by features unique to Russia's history and pattern of development, which deserve mention in order to view the contemporary conflict of systems in perspective.

The Broad Perspective

The Soviet Union represents a peculiar Western variant. While sharing some of the roots of the Western world, the development of the Russian people followed a decidedly different course. They did not experience a Renaissance, a Reformation, or an Enlightenment. There was in their history no tradition of chivalry and *noblesse oblige* to restrain the forces of political absolutism. Historically, Russians have admired much of Western culture. The efforts of Peter the Great and Catherine the Great to emulate the West attest to this attraction. But the very method by which Western ideas were transferred and implanted in Russia bespoke a non-Western tradition. Totalitarian methods were linked to a Western import—Marxian ideology—to provide the motive power for the Soviet Union's modernization. The Soviet state has heavily filtered the values of the West. Materialism has been accepted; the Judeo-Christian ethic, rejected. Technology has been accepted; humanism and political liberalism, rejected. Yet Western impulses remain strong and persistent, even in the Soviet Union.

In today's conflict of systems the Soviet Union confronts the dynamism of the Western world—the truly revolutionary force of the modern age. Unable to match the power of the West, the Soviet Union has adopted tactics designed to delay and, if possible, disrupt greater integration of Western peoples. Viewed in this perspective, Soviet strategy vis-à-vis the West is two-pronged: first, a negative and reactive stand against the liberalizing influences of the Western world; second, a hostile and offensive drive to broaden the power base of the Soviet Union.

There are many ironic twists in the East-West confrontation. The U.S.S.R., harnessed to its archaic Marxist ideology, employs conflict techniques which are aggressive and power-oriented. The West, possessing attributes which give it every reason for taking the ideological offensive, appears not to recognize the revolutionary power and appeal of its "way of life" and has employed essentially reactive tactics in its defense against communism. In short, the West possesses the material power but lacks the ideological fervor and psychopolitical insight with which to exploit the many weaknesses of communism.

Historical Background of Communism in the Americas

At the time of the Bolshevik Revolution, those areas of Latin America which had experienced the effects of the Industrial Revolution had already had a history of political radicalism. Some Latin American syndicalists, anarchists, and socialists found inspiration in the Russian Revolution. Their past efforts at radical political reform frustrated, many began to believe that the Communist movement possessed the ideological drive and the revolutionary techniques which would assure success. The attraction of elements of the Latin American radical Left to the Russian Revolution was stimulated in the years after 1917 by the extensive travels of such Comintern agents as the Indian

Manabendra Nath Roy and the Japanese socialist Sen Katayama.

The first Communist party in Latin America was founded in Argentina in 1918. In succeeding years Communist parties were established in Chile, Uruguay, Brazil, and Mexico. A Lithuanian Communist who used the name Guralsky and made Buenos Aires his headquarters was the first permanent representative of the Comintern in Latin America.[1] The establishment of Soviet embassies in Montevideo in 1922 and Mexico City in 1924 facilitated the work of the Comintern. By 1924 the Comintern had decided to create a Latin American Secretariat. The establishment in 1926 of the Lenin Institute in Moscow, a training center in the techniques of revolution, gave impetus to the Communist movement in Latin America. By the mid-1920s Latin American Communist parties were promoting strikes and other disturbances. This new militancy increased after the Sixth Comintern Congress, held in Moscow in 1928. In the following year the first Latin American regional Communist party congress was held in Buenos Aires.

Despite their revolutionary fervor, the early activities of Latin American Communists produced no notable successes throughout the 1920s and the first half of the 1930s. Apparently the Soviets had little understanding of the Latin American environment. Moreover, the initial enthusiasm generated during the early years of Communist party organization soon gave way to unimaginative bureaucratic control. Seen in global perspective, Latin America still held low priority in the view of Soviet tacticians.

In the mid-1930s a profound tactical debate gripped the Communist movement. It contributed to the postponement of the Seventh Comintern Congress scheduled in Moscow in 1934 and resounded within Latin American Communist parties. Of the many issues under debate, one of the most important was: Should communism pursue its ends by direct revolutionary action, or should it follow the tactics of political maneuver to achieve nonviolent take-over? Manuilsky, an old Stalin hand, advocated the first course of action. Dimitrov, then rising to leadership

---

[1] Victor Alba, *Historia del comunismo en América latina,* Ediciones Occidentales, Mexico City, 1960, pp. 21, 36.

within the Comintern, favored the second course of action. The heat of the tactical debate was all the greater by virtue of the history of the dispute between Stalin and Trotsky in the mid-1920s and the subsequent tactical debate between Stalin and Mao Tse-tung following the Communist debacle of 1927 in China. Stalin favored adoption of both tactics, with emphasis to be placed upon the one which appeared to offer the best possibilities of success in a given situation. Stalin's view prevailed and, despite recurring debates, his tactical pragmatism guided the operational code of communism.

The dual tactical orientation adopted by the Comintern during the mid-1930s was reflected in Latin America in the contrasting programs pursued by the Communist parties of Brazil and Chile. Luis Carlos Prestes, leader of the Brazilian Communist Party, developed plans for a military putsch. Meanwhile, Eudocio Ravines (a Peruvian by birth but then heading the Comintern's activities in Chile) formed a popular-front movement in Chile.

The Prestes putsch of November 1935 ended in dismal failure, whereas Ravines' efforts to form a popular front in Chile resulted in successful penetration of labor and university education and the building of a "respectable" image for the Chilean Communist Party which has endured to this day. International events led the Communists to a general adoption of the popular-front tactic during the mid-1930s, since it was well suited to protecting the interests of the Soviet Union at a time when the menace of Nazi Germany loomed on the horizon.[2]

Communism in Latin America was strengthened during the late 1930s by the influx of Communists among the Spanish Republicans who had fled before Franco's victory in Spain. Many Spanish Communists provided useful organizational skills and operational experience. The biggest boost to Communist fortunes in Latin America, however, came from World War II. The war enabled the Soviet Union to pose as a worthy ally of the Western Powers and provided Communists throughout Latin America with an opportunity to masquerade as loyal citizens supporting

[2] Eudocio Ravines, *The Yenan Way*, Charles Scribner's Sons, New York, 1951, pp. 164–174. Ravines' description of the united front tactic—which he terms the Yenan Way—is of particular interest.

the fight against the Axis Powers. Communism in Latin America achieved a high point in its development during the years 1945–1946. Many of the Communist parties were given legal status, which enabled them to participate in parliamentary politics. In Brazil, the Communists polled nearly one million votes in 1947, electing two senators, fourteen deputies, and more than sixty representatives to state legislatures.[3] Communists also held seats in the congresses of Cuba, Bolivia, Chile, Colombia, Costa Rica, Ecuador, and Uruguay during this period, and three party members held cabinet posts in the Chilean government. The Communists increased their strength among intellectual, labor, and student groups throughout the hemisphere.

Despite advances during and immediately following World War II, the Communist movement was unable to capitalize on its sudden success. In contrast, non-Communist revolutionary efforts such as the Mexican Revolution, the Alianza Popular Revolucionaria Americana (APRA) organization of Peru, the Peronista movement in Argentina, and the Movimiento Nacional Revolucionario (MNR) party of Bolivia either had achieved success or at least had penetrated more deeply than had the Communists in the countries concerned. Some Latin American Communist parties overplayed their hands. Growing Soviet aggressiveness toward the West weakened the effectiveness of the popular-front tactic. Communist opportunism in the phase of the popular-front tactic had made enemies. The Communist movement was also hampered by favorable economic conditions throughout Latin America during the late 1940s and early 1950s. In addition, the United States was beginning to have at least limited success in alerting Latin America to the Communist menace and in building an inter-American defense against Communist infiltration and subversion. By 1952 much of the mass wartime support won by Latin American Communist parties was lost, and the fortunes of communism in the Americas waned.

Loss of support by Latin American Communist parties during the late 1940s and early 1950s did not, however, radically weaken the strength of party cadres—the well-indoctrinated and

[3] D. A. Graber, *Crisis Diplomacy*, Public Affairs Press, Washington, D.C., 1959, p. 241.

disciplined elite membership. The loss of the hangers-on acquired in the years of popularity did not cripple the Communists, for they had never depended upon mass membership. The
resilience of the Communist movement was demonstrated dramatically by its infiltration of the Arévalo Government in Guatemala between 1946 and 1950 and its dominance in the Arbenz
regime which followed. Communist success in Guatemala revealed once again the effectiveness of slow and patient infiltration tactics. Only an anti-Communist revolutionary movement in
1954, aided and supported by the United States, prevented
Guatemala from becoming the first Soviet satellite in the Western Hemisphere.

Although denied victory in Guatemala, Latin American Communists had learned many valuable lessons, and by the mid-
1950s the winds in many places were again blowing in favor of
their cause. Many factors accounted for this turn of events. For
one, the beginning of systematic Soviet study of Latin America
resulted in a more astute diagnosis of the vulnerabilities of Latin
American society. (In 1953 the Soviet Academy of Sciences established a section devoted to Latin America.) On balance,
however, it was not so much Soviet effort as the growing Latin
American demand for radical solutions which abetted the Communist offensive during the latter half of the 1950s.

Over three centuries of Iberian rule tended to develop in Latin
Americans a colonial mentality, a feeling which has been per-
petuated by continuing economic dependence upon external
centers of power. A sense of stagnation has created a psychological *ambiente* ready-made for antiforeign agitation. Self-pity and
frustration have been important ingredients of this pathology. In
brief, the very failure of Latin America to advance more rapidly
and become a more integral part of the modern West has made
it vulnerable to Communist exploitation.

Imbued with idealism, Latin American youth in great numbers
have rejected and rebelled against traditional societies which
continue to condone corruption and inefficiency and to resist
change. A sense of injustice and a quest for greater freedom have
inspired political radicalism. The result has been a rising surge

of *jacobinismo* and *populismo*.[4] These currents of unrest have
been fed by other factors: a population explosion unaccompa-
nied by proportionate growth in economic opportunity, a mass
exodus from rural to urban areas ill-prepared to employ productively unskilled labor, and continued dependence upon the fluc-
tuating proceeds of primary-product exports. It is not surprising
that a sense of frustration combines with a feeling of neglect to
feed ultranationalist forces. The hypersensitivity of many Latin
Americans to any semblance of foreign intervention provides
numerous targets for Soviet propaganda.

Soviet programs in the economic and scientific fields have im-
pressed Latin Americans, many of whom assume that Soviet
organizational and planning techniques provide an answer to
any backward country's drive for industrialization. The revolutionary image which the Soviets project has appealed to Latin
American youth. Young people are increasingly impatient with
what they feel to be perfunctory bureaucracies that impede
rather than advance popular demands. Furthermore, Soviet offers of trade to economies which are hard pressed to find markets
for excess primary products are tempting.

Despite Latin America's vulnerabilities to communism, some
important countervailing forces have been at work. The Iberian
commitment to *dignidad* and individualism does not lend itself
to the discipline and regimentation of Communist organizational
methods. Long acceptance of a stratified social order has made
it difficult for the Communists to ignite class warfare. In addition, Iberian transcendentalism does not easily accommodate itself to the atheism and crass materialism of communism or the
arrogance and opportunism so often displayed by its leaders.
The record of Latin American institutional elements as bulwarks
against communism has been mixed; but the church and the
military, at various times and places, have helped to defend
against Communist take-over.

Another factor which has impeded the progress of communism
in the Americas has been the mediocre quality of some of its

[4] For a discussion of the trend toward political radicalism, specifically the
type often labeled *jacobinismo*, see chap. 5.

leadership. Many Latin American Communist leaders have displayed a genius for promoting their own welfare, even to the extent of choosing underlings who are unlikely to challenge their leadership. They have also frequently become absorbed in the minutiae of methodology—a tendency which has encouraged bureaucratic ossification within Communist ranks.

Soviet moves on the international front have sometimes required embarrassing shifts in the positions of Latin American Communist parties. At times this has resulted in damaging defections and a splintering of party organizations. The Nazi-Soviet Pact of 1939, the Soviet suppression of the Hungarian revolution in 1956, the denigration of Stalin, the Cuban missile crisis of 1962, and the Sino-Soviet conflict are cases in point. Other Soviet shifts—such as those requiring Latin American parties to abandon old positions and adopt new alliances, to work with dictators while maintaining an antidictatorial façade, to sabotage yesterday's allies for today's opportunism—have affected adversely party fortunes. In the economic sphere, Latin American Communists are confronted with the fact that the Soviet Union and Communist China can offer Latin America few real alternative market possibilities to those that are currently available in North America and Western Europe.

In spite of these countervailing influences, Latin American Communists have generally been adept operationally. By the exercise of superior tactics and organization, the Communists attempt to minimize their weaknesses and maximize those of the society they seek to subvert. An understanding of Communist tactics is essential to an assessment of the danger they pose.

Nature of the Communist Movement

The Communist movement is power-oriented, with its strength resting largely on superior operational tactics and organization. The advance of communism has depended greatly upon highly developed conflict techniques in the hands of trained, disciplined, and indoctrinated revolutionaries. Being an elite-oriented rather than mass-oriented movement, the strength and danger of the Communists can be measured neither by the number of their adherents nor by the electoral appeal of its parties. Communist party organizations form but part of its international force. The Soviet state apparatus plays a less known, heavily veiled, but highly significant role in the Communist movement's drive for power. The term "Soviet state apparatus" embraces the many instrumentalities available to the U.S.S.R. for supporting and guiding Communist movements abroad. Soviet intelligence arms such as the KGB and GRU (Russian initials for Committee of State Security and Chief Intelligence Directorate, respectively) form the conspiratorial segment of the state apparatus. Many Soviet diplomatic personnel—even those not serving in an intelligence capacity—would regard covert political action as part of the Soviet embassy's normal functions. The Soviet Academy (to be discussed subsequently) helps to chart the strategy of the Communist movement; in this role it, too, is part of the Soviet state apparatus.

Communist ideology, to the perceptive critic, is a collection of tired slogans woven into a dogma which time and the progress of human events have proved invalid. This has not prevented the Communist elite from using ideology to fire the enthusiasm of followers or sympathizers unable to discern its demonstrated anachronisms and inadequacies. The ideology has also served to guide the actions of party cadres. A deceptively simple interpretation of world events, Marxism-Leninism is the opiate of the unsophisticated. In this sense, Communist ideology is a potent force—particularly because of its appeal to those who see in the writings of Marx and Lenin a description of social conditions they can identify as similar to those of their backward or traditional societies. Believing the Marxian diagnoses applicable to their own problems, some Latin Americans are led to conclude that Marxian prescriptions may also be valid, *despite* evidence to to the contrary offered by the historical experience of the modern West and of the Soviet Union itself. Thus, to the Communist elite, the Marxist-Leninist ideology is a useful tool in the advance of their cause.

The Communist movement, even though it be far from monolithic and tending toward polycentrism, clearly serves the purposes of the Soviet Union. Moscow's control over individual

party organizations in Latin America varies. But complete sub-
servience to the Soviet Union has long been considered by Moscow as both unrealistic and unnecessary. Herein lies the importance of the Soviet state apparatus. Through its channels Moscow
maintains control of key party functionaries as well as persons
who are not party members but who nevertheless serve the
Soviet cause.

Contrary to its pretensions of being a movement of the masses,
communism in fact regards the masses as expendable in carefully
managed conflicts designed to forward Communist objectives
without subjecting its leadership to undue risks. Rather than
having a real concern for the masses, the Communist movement
concentrates on certain key groups. In Latin America three such
groups are the intellectuals, university students, and labor. Infiltration of the first two groups provides leadership and motive
power. Labor is the expendable mass which provides the operational leverage for paralyzing the economic life of a target society. Concentration on the above three target groups does not,
of course, mean that other operational possibilities are neglected.
Key governmental bureaus are also prime targets for Communist
penetration. In some Latin American countries even the military
has been infiltrated by Communists. Communist propaganda
makes much of its defense of the landless peasant, but in reality
the peasant, the rural counterpart of the urban worker, is also
regarded as expendable. Communist plans are not built upon
continued allegiance of the peasant but rather on use of the
peasant to destroy the *latifundista*.

Major Techniques

In pursuing their objectives the Communists employ a number
of techniques, of which the most important are deception, agitation, and propaganda.

Deception is basic to the operations of a conspiratorial movement. It has been aptly said that the Communists "interfere in
the name of noninterference, and wage war in the name of
peace." [5] The statements of Communist Cuba's leaders show how

[5] William R. Kintner and Joseph Z. Kornfeder, *The New Frontier of War*,
Henry Regnery Company, Chicago, 1962, p. xvii.

the deception technique is employed. During the early days of the revolution, Ernesto "Che" Guevara admonished those present at a secret meeting to remember not to repeat what had been said because "at these meetings, we talk about what we are going to do, and not what we tell the people we are going to do. These are seldom the same thing." [6] In his speech of December 2, 1961, Fidel Castro openly admitted the deception he had perpetrated earlier on his non-Communist followers:

> ... because otherwise we might have alienated the bourgeoisie and other forces which we knew we would eventually have to fight.... If it were known then that the men who led the guerrilla fighting had radical ideas, well all those who are making war against us now would have started it right then. [7]

A wide variety of agitation operations spearhead Communist attacks. At times agitation seeks a psychological effect: to instill confusion, fear, guilt, and defeatism within non-Communist societies. Agitation is also aimed at aggravating class frictions and racial problems, as well as exacerbating popular dissatisfaction of all kinds. Another agitation tactic seeks to generate hope among the "outs" or impoverished masses—often groundless or exaggerated hope—with the calculation that ensuing disappointment will exert pressure upon constituted authorities and hasten their downfall.

Perhaps the oldest and certainly the most highly developed arm of the Communist movement's deception and agitation operations is propaganda. Among the media used by the Communist movement in Latin America are the press, radio, films, and literature. Cultural exchange programs and friendship societies serve as useful vehicles for propaganda, as do the subsidized visits to Communist countries of prominent, sympathetic politicians. Communist propaganda stresses "Yankee imperialism and exploitation," and Latin America's nationalistic feelings are stirred up by charges of "Yankee intervention." The Organization of American States is a major target. In recent years, the Alliance for Progress has drawn much of the Communist fire, the basic aim being one of sowing defeatism along with suspicion as to the

[6] Manuel Artime Buesa, *Traición!* Editorial Jus, Mexico City, 1960, p. 64.
[7] *The New York Times,* Dec. 3, 1961.

good faith and intentions of the United States. A brand of *latino-americanismo* that cannot be harmonized with Pan-American ideals of hemispheric solidarity is encouraged to give aspirations for regional unity a decided anti–United States flavor. As their principal internal targets the Communists concentrate on the Latin American military and the *latifundistas*.

Clever interweaving of these various themes—combined with ancillary deception and agitation operations—make up the Communist attempt to achieve the *basic objective of Soviet strategy in the Americas, i.e., the prevention of Latin America's closer identification and integration with the modern West*. Since the prospects for applying direct Soviet military power in the Americas are presently remote, Communist "conflict operations" in Latin America have concentrated on political and economic warfare.

The Communists constantly raise the charge of "economic imperialism." Communist economic warfare encourages the confiscation of foreign properties and investments without adequate compensation. It promotes broad nationalization schemes, regardless of the ability of the target country to manage the programs advanced. The objective of these moves is to prevent Latin America's orderly economic growth and closer cooperation with the North Atlantic nations. To advance this broad objective, the Soviet Union complements the actions of local Communist parties with offers of financial credits, technical assistance, and expanded trade.

Other actions pursued by local Communist parties are designed to hinder Latin America's sound development. Irresponsible plans of agrarian reform are advanced with the alleged aim of helping the landless peasant but with the real object of destroying the *latifundista* and extending the influence and control of the Party over the peasants. Ambitious social welfare programs are supported even though it is clear that the state's resources are inadequate to bear the costs. Lower consumer prices are demanded on the one hand while unsound fiscal policies which result in rampant inflation are pushed on the other. Through the clever interweaving of Communist conflict techniques, political and economic warfare is conducted to achieve the disruption and eventual breakdown of the target society. Naturally, it is hoped that the ensuing chaos will provide conditions for the assumption of power by a disciplined, highly trained, and well-organized Communist elite.

Major Tactical Lines

Throughout its history communism has employed—singly or together—two broad tactical lines: the united front and direct action for revolutionary overthrow. These two basic tactics have been described in various ways. Consequently the terminology employed—particularly the term "united front"—must be interpreted broadly. The united-front concept as used here has been stretched to include Lenin's concept of the "bourgeois democratic revolution"; the popular-front coalitions which joined Communist and democratic parties during the late 1930s and World War II years; and the "national liberation front," which is the currently favored name for the amalgamation of the radical Left. The direct-action tactic as employed here is intended to cover all forms of violence aimed at revolutionary overthrow, i.e., guerrilla warfare, sabotage, various forms of terror, and assassination.

The united-front tactic was generally adopted by the Communists during the mid-1930s and maintained throughout the years of World War II. This tactic has generally met with greater success in Latin America than the alternative direct-action approach. It has been pursued for many years by the Chilean Communist Party but achieved only temporary, though notable, success in Guatemala when, in 1954, Communist control was established during the Arbenz regime. It seems likely that the united front will continue to be a major Communist tactic even though its success has only been qualified. The united front in which the Chilean Communists now participate—Frente de Acción Popular (FRAP)—continues the policy introduced by Ravines almost three decades ago. Communist efforts in Argentina to arrive at a working relationship with the Peronistas reveal a similar but less successful use of the united front. The National Liberation Front, to which the Communist Party of Brazil gave strong support prior to Goulart's ouster by the Brazilian military, provides another example of the appeal which the united front continues to hold for Latin American Communists. Pursuit of this tactic does not mean, however, that the Communists have abandoned the use of direct action when conditions for this alternative tactic appear favorable.

The history of the Communist movement in Latin America is replete with instances of violent agitation. Unlike protest movements which have a more limited objective, some forms of Communist agitation clearly seek to produce revolutionary political change. A limited number of Communist-directed putsches, such as that led by Prestes in Brazil in 1935, has taken place. By and large, the violent agitation and putschist activities of Latin American Communists have not been successful. More often they have produced strong counteraction resulting in repression of Communist activities. This history of failure does not mean that the Communists of Latin America have abandoned the direct-action approach. If anything, there are indications that the use of this tactic is on the increase.

The terrorist and guerrilla activity launched by the Communist-dominated Armed Forces of National Liberation (Fuerzas Armadas de la Liberación Nacional—FALN) in Venezuela received a setback when the Communists were unable to sabotage the presidential elections of December 1963. Ninety-six per cent of the eligible voters of Venezuela went to the polls in spite of the FALN threat to kill anyone appearing near the polling places. Energetic action enabled the Betancourt government to thwart the direct-action tactics of the Communists.

Despite the FALN's setback, the Venezuelan Communists show no signs of giving up their campaign of violence. Early in 1964 some elements of the Venezuelan Communist Party advocated at least temporary abandonment of direct-action tactics, apparently in the hope that a "soft line" would win amnesty for Party leaders then imprisoned. That this represented a temporary tactic is supported by the fact that in November 1963 approximately three tons of smuggled arms were discovered in a coastal area of Venezuela. At the request of the Venezuelan government, an OAS investigative committee was appointed to review Betancourt's charge that the arms could be traced to Communist

Cuba. In February 1964 this committee, following a thorough review of the case, substantiated the Venezuelan government's charge and accused the Castro regime of aggression against Venezuela. The FALN has continued to receive support from Communist Cuba and the Soviet state apparatus.

Early in 1965 Communist couriers were apprehended in Caracas after an unsuccessful effort to deliver Soviet funds to the Venezuelan Communist Party and the FALN. Captured Venezuelan Communist Party documents and the public statements of Venezuelan Communist leaders indicate that the FALN will continue to wage a campaign of guerrilla warfare, infiltration of the Venezuelan military, and urban terrorism. Incipient guerrilla activities in Guatemala, the Dominican Republic, Colombia, Peru, Ecuador, and Honduras suggest that the direct-action formula may be applied increasingly in the years to come.

The Communists have long been adept at merging direct action with the activities of united-front groups. They do not regard these tactics as mutually exclusive but as complementary routes to power. Thus, the Communists hope that the increased operational flexibility provided by a skillful combination of the united-front and the direct-action tactics will permit them to achieve their objectives with more subtlety and finesse. The merger of the united-front and direct-action tactics can be illustrated by no better example than the Cuban revolution led by Fidel Castro.

Under Castro's leadership the 26th of July Movement served as a united front. The movement combined a variety of anti-Batista elements—the majority of which were members of a democratically oriented Cuban middle class—and devised a program which was moderate in tone and revealed no connection with communism. Fidel Castro took great care not to associate himself or the movement with the Cuban Communist Party. This tactic bolstered his image as a moderate revolutionary, thus broadening his base of political support. Castro's guerrilla movement provided the direct-action element. The chief function of the guerrillas was to create a heroic Robin Hood image around which anti-Batista forces could coalesce. From a military point of view, Castro's guerrillas were little more than a nuisance to the Batista regime. Castro himself stated that his guerrilla forces numbered not more than 180 men in April 1953, after sixteen months of struggle. At the end of December 1958—on the eve of victory—Castro's forces numbered approximately 800 men. Batista's failure to eliminate the guerrillas during the early days of Sierra Maestra proved to be a grave tactical error—more from a psychological than a military point of view.

During the revolutionary struggle, the Cuban Communist Party was left in Castro's wake, although its less spectacular tactics of infiltration, agitation, and propaganda undoubtedly contributed to Batista's downfall. The usual opportunistic political course of the Communist Party of Cuba was continued during the rule of Batista and facilitated Communist infiltration of the regime. While some party members were ostensibly political allies of Batista, others worked for the dictator's overthrow, particularly after mid-1958 when his grip began to weaken. This dual orientation gave the Communists great flexibility of action. The Party attempted to build up popular resentment to the point where coordinated action of the peasant and urban worker might make direct action for Batista's ouster feasible. The Party never achieved this objective, however, and its active agitation efforts ended in dismal failure.

With the Communist Party playing a secondary role, Castro was successful in projecting himself into a position of undisputed leadership of the revolution. The interweaving of the united-front and direct-action tactics provided the formula for Castro's success. How can the variant tactics followed by Castro and the Cuban Communist Party be explained and reconciled? This question is best approached by examining an important but neglected facet of the Cuban Revolution, namely, *the operational role played by the Soviet state apparatus.*

Soviet Political Action

Considerable confusion has attended many of the explanations of Communist victory in Cuba. Debate continues as to whether Fidel Castro and his principal lieutenants are *really* Communists. Another issue centers on the separate but parallel courses followed by Castro's 26th of July Movement and the Cuban Communist Party, leading to the question as to whether these two approaches were really separate and independent or simply integrated parts of a grandiose deception plan. Debate also persists as to whether the apparent cleavage between Castro and the "old guard" of the Cuban Communist Party is real or notional.

From his youth, Castro dabbled in Marxian literature, toyed with political radicalism, and cultivated a supreme ego. From this background many conjectures can be drawn. It is conceivable that Fidel Castro has not been and is not today a member of the Cuban Communist Party in any orthodox sense, although his purposes and those of the Cuban Party might now be served by "establishing" this identification. Castro's speech of December 2, 1961, contained the clear admission that he had been throughout the revolution and would forever remain a Marxist-Leninist. However, having revealed his deception in one breath, it is not unlikely that his admission may also have shielded an ulterior motive.

There is overwhelming evidence to support the conclusion that the separate but parallel courses followed by Castro's 26th of July Movement and the Cuban Communist Party were not part of a purposeful deception plan, although confusion among anti-Communist forces within Cuba as well as abroad was clearly one of the results achieved. These separate courses were born of the struggle for power within the revolutionary forces of the Left. *These two contending revolutionary currents were joined by the Soviet state apparatus. The Soviets used this apparatus to guide and manipulate both revolutionary factions and provided, in effect, the subterranean passage which linked them even in their rivalry for power.* The apparent cleavage between Castro and some of the "old guard" of the Cuban Communist Party may simply reflect a power struggle within the Communist movement —an event not uncommon.

Although documentation for interpreting the course of the Cuban revolution is lacking, it seems evident that the Soviet Union was attracted early in the 1950s, if not before, by the operational potential of Fidel Castro and other Cubans of the radical Left. It is possible that Ernesto "Che" Guevara was the principal link between the Soviets and Fidel Castro. There is much in "Che" Guevara's background—his previous activities as a professional revolutionary and his apparently deep Marxist-Leninist convictions—which suggests that he served as the brains of a Soviet-directed revolutionary operation in Cuba.[8] This operation offered the Soviets an alternative to the revolutionary program pursued by the Cuban Communist Party. When and under what terms Fidel Castro cast his lot with the Soviet-directed revolutionary effort must remain for the present a matter of speculation. The Soviets, not overly concerned with Castro's ideology, were attracted by his charismatic personality which was useful in tightening the Communist grip on the revolutionary movement.

Castro remains an enigma in many ways. His deepest motives and ultimate course may be as much a matter of speculation in Moscow as they are in Washington. Castro is clearly not simply a Soviet "stooge," nor can Castro's Cuba be classified as "just another Soviet satellite." But the Soviet Union does not play its cards loosely. It is reasonable to assume that Moscow's heavy investment in Cuba has been adequately protected by others who are ready and willing to preserve the Soviet Union's "equity" —with or without Castro. The polycentric trend of international communism which the Soviets have been forced to accept since the demise of Stalin has provided Castro tactical latitude but can hardly be expected to grant him real freedom of action. Castro has clearly delivered the Cuban revolution to communism. Should Moscow feel its ability to "pull the strings" seriously impeded, Castro may well be considered expendable.

Many of the debates which surround the Communist take-over of the Cuban revolution are essentially irrelevant to the design of Communist strategy and tactics in the Americas. Fidel Castro today as in the past—whatever his motivation might be—serves the interest of the Soviet Union. This is the essential point on which the Americas must focus and take action, for there are

---

[8] "Che" Guevara's reported departure from Cuba in April 1965, together with his apparent disagreement with current Soviet revolutionary strategy, is not necessarily inconsistent with the thesis that he played a key role in a Soviet-directed political-action operation in the 1950s with Cuba as its target. Factionalism among revolutionaries is a common occurence.

other potential Fidel Castros in Latin America. Attempts to identify them must *not* be rigidly focused on Latin American Communist parties alone or on the front groups they control. The Soviets, especially their conspiratorial component, have demonstrated a considerable capability for spotting, training, and lending operational support to those individuals believed to have a potential for forwarding the interests of the Soviet Union. The party labels they wear are essentially unimportant. Moreover, their possible opposition to local Communist party leadership, whether real or notional, may well enhance their utility to the Soviets rather than diminish it.

Communist parties in Latin America are important but by no means the only tools for achieving Soviet objectives. Herein lies the significance of the activities of the Soviet state apparatus. Some elements of the Latin American radical Left *not* identified with Communist movements represent a serious challenge to the defense of the Americas. Unlike identified Communists, they can masquerade as true nationalists and patriots. They can draw upon the support of many Left-wing socialists and others influenced by Marxian philosophy and act as catalysts for the organization of national liberation fronts.

The operational flexibility which these possibilities offer to the Soviets constitutes an intriguing yet little known side of the Communist movement in Latin America today. The concern it should evoke is heightened by the fact that new Soviet diplomatic installations in Latin America have provided additional bases for Soviet operations. Prior to the Cuban revolution, the Soviet embassies were confined to Mexico City, Montevideo, and Buenos Aires. Now Havana, Brasilia, and Santiago have been added. In addition the Soviet Union no doubt makes full use of those operational bases provided by the diplomatic and commercial installations maintained by Cuba and East European satellites.

Ambassador Edwin M. Martin, when Assistant Secretary of State for Inter-American Affairs, stated that in 1962 between 1,000 and 1,500 Latin Americans traveled to Cuba for ideological indoctrination or guerrilla-warfare training.[9] The flow of Latin

---

[9] *Department of State Bulletin,* Mar. 11, 1963, pp. 350–351.

American trainees to Cuba is continuing. The School of Latin American Studies in Prague is another important training center which has been in operation since the early 1950s. Most of the students attending the Prague school are Latin Americans, but a number of Soviet bloc diplomats slated for assignments in Latin America are trained with them. Once in Latin America they work in teams.[10]

Within the U.S.S.R. itself the Higher Party School under the Central Committee in Moscow has trained hundreds of Communist leaders, many of them from Latin America. In February 1962 the Soviet Academy of Sciences founded a Latin American Institute which probably serves as a high-level staff for the analysis and planning of operations conducted by the Soviets in Latin America. The Soviet Ministry of Foreign Affairs has established a Latin American Department. A society of Soviet-Ibero-American Friendship has been founded. These developments point to an increased Soviet effort in Latin America and illustrate the multiple facilities available to the Soviet Union for the pursuit of Communist objectives in Latin America.

Brazil, during the administration of João Goulart, was a showcase of Communist strategy and tactics at work. Brazilian Communists used a variety of operational techniques including agitation, propaganda, and deception. Directly and through front organizations, the Communist Party of Brazil (PCB) had infiltrated over the years many intellectual, student, and labor groups. The Communists tried to inflame popular dissatisfaction, weaken opposition to a radical political course of action, and fragment the Brazilian military, which posed the most formidable obstacle to their revolutionary efforts.

An active propaganda campaign supplemented the divisive and agitational activities of the Party and its front organizations. The PCB launched a major campaign against alleged foreign economic exploitation in an attempt to discourage continued foreign investment and contribute to the disruption of Brazil's economy. The Communists advocated broad and sweeping

[10] Josef Kalvoda, "Communist Strategy in Latin America," *Yale Review*, Autumn 1960, pp. 36–37; Daniel James, *Red Design for the Americas*, The John Day Company, Inc., New York: 1954, pp. 202–203.

schemes of nationalization which far exceeded the administrative abilities of the Brazilian government, as well as its resources for compensation of the owners of expropriated properties. The Party combined a denunciation of higher costs of living with advocacy of policies which contributed to Brazil's rampant inflation.

The PCB used the National Liberation Front—an ultranationalist organization which the Communists had heavily infiltrated—to harness the revolutionary potential of crypto-Communists, Party sympathizers, and Leftist ultranationalists with varied political affiliations. The National Liberation Front strongly advocated radical measures and pushed its agitational activities to a point where they bordered upon revolutionary action. Meanwhile the Secretary General of the Brazilian Communist Party, Luis Carlos Prestes, expressed Moscow's line of "peaceful coexistence" while pursuing parliamentary tactics and attempting to achieve legal status for the PCB. Thus the Communists combined united-front and direct-action tactics in order to create chaos and confusion, and eventually engineer a revolutionary overthrow.

The domestic agitation and propaganda of the PCB were supplemented by activities designed to loosen Brazil's ties with the West. Communist support of an "independent" Brazilian foreign policy cloaked an attempt to weaken Brazil's hemispheric ties and create opposition to United States objectives both within the inter-American system as well as on extrahemispheric issues. Soviet propaganda efforts aided in the pursuit of this PCB objective by pronouncements, such as those made at the Geneva World Trade and Development Conference in 1964, which claimed to champion the cause of underdeveloped countries. The Soviets, for example, purported to favor the efforts of primary-commodity producers to obtain better prices on the international market and thus overcome the "stranglehold" which the advanced "capitalistic nations of the West" have supposedly maintained. The Soviets obviously had Brazil as well as other Latin American nations in mind when they formulated this propaganda line.

From the sidelines, shielded operations of the Soviet state apparatus attempted to prepare a revolutionary climate within

Brazil, especially during the last year of Goulart's Presidency. The Communist Party in Brazil represented only one instrument of Soviet political action. With their well-developed and flexible operational techniques, the Soviets no doubt employed all their ingenuity to link the varied efforts of such apparently diverse elements as the orthodox PCB, headed by Luis Carlos Prestes, who preached a line of peaceful coexistence; the dissident members of the PCB who are in open opposition to Prestes and advocated revolutionary tactics; Francisco Julião, a federal deputy, active in agitating and organizing the rural peasants in Brazil's Northeast; and Leonel Brizola, another federal deputy who followed an opportunistic and demagogic line of political radicalism and attempted to unite revolutionary elements within the National Liberation Front. Sensing the weakness in Brazil's social fabric, the Soviet Union tried to exploit to the fullest the crisis through which Brazil passed during the final months of João Goulart's administration.

The Communist threat precipitated, early in April 1964, the Brazilian military's ouster of Goulart and crackdown on PCB revolutionaries and their allies. For the time, at least, the Communist cause in Brazil has received a setback, but it can be expected that the PCB and the Soviets will try to recover their strength and exploit future possibilities for undermining Brazilian society. Even in failure, the subversive attempt of the Communists in Brazil illustrates the adroit interweaving of varied techniques and political tactics of which the PCB and Soviet Union are capable.

The Sino-Soviet Rift

The aggressiveness of the Castro regime, and the revolutionary program it advocates elsewhere in Latin America, is sometimes linked with discussions of the Sino-Soviet tactical conflict which has attracted so much interest in recent years. Contrary to many current interpretations, there is no need for reconciliation between Castro's call for revolution and Moscow's advocacy of peaceful coexistence. Just as the Cuban revolution combined with great finesse both united-front and direct-action tactics,

Moscow and Peking have advocated a variety of tactical approaches that include the same operational spectrum. It would be incorrect to believe that Moscow is opposed to violent revolution in Latin America today.[11] From the Soviet point of view, peaceful coexistence is designed to provide an atmosphere within which the class struggle can be pursued more effectively rather than abandoned. Alternatively, Peking's revolutionary fervor has not in the past precluded its advocacy of the peaceful united-front approach. No doubt both Moscow and Peking will continue to use a great variety of tactics to suit their interpretations of the objective reality, i.e., to serve their respective interests.

The Sino-Soviet rift has caused appreciable difficulty within many Latin American Communist parties. Serious disputes have erupted, and the Communist parties of some Latin American countries have split openly into competitive pro-Moscow and pro-Peking factions. Where these difficulties will lead is a matter of conjecture. The preceding pages have deliberately emphasized the impact of *Moscow*-directed communism in the Americas, since *Peking*-directed communism has had too brief a history to record and too recent and spotty a presence to evaluate. It is quite conceivable that the Chinese Communists may increase their influence significantly in the years ahead. Certainly this is Peking's objective, judging by its propaganda and organizational activities, and by the energies it has devoted to training selected Latin American Communist party leaders in Communist China. As of the mid-1960s, however, it would appear that Moscow's resources, experience, and superior logistics place the U.S.S.R. in a better position than the Chinese Communists in Latin America. Little comfort can be taken by the United States or the West in general as a result of the competitive efforts of Moscow and Peking in Latin America, since both "brands" of com-

[11] A meeting of all Latin American Communist parties at which Soviet representatives were in attendance reportedly took place in Havana in November 1964. Moscow radio announced on January 18, 1965 that this meeting resulted in the acceptance of Castro's doctrine of violent revolution, provided such movements are conducted (with some exceptions) through local Communist party organizations and confined to areas where revolutionary success appeared most promising.

munism are determined to prevent Latin America's integration within an Atlantic Community of the West. The future strength of communism in Latin America will, nonetheless, depend in large part on the ability of Moscow and Peking to harmonize the activities of their respective adherents in the region. Consequently, developments in the Sino-Soviet rift, as reflected in Latin America, will continue to be of great import.

Summary Appraisal

Efforts to discover *the* formula being applied by the Communists in Latin America today will be found neither by the study of Sino-Soviet "tactical debates" nor by disputes as to whether or not Fidel Castro is a Communist. The lesson is simple: *The Communist formula calls for identifying, gaining control of, and giving direction to those power groups which serve the cause and forward the objectives of the Soviet Union (or Communist China).* The tactical flexibility which this formula demands will at times call for Soviet (or Chinese Communist) support to widely divergent and even conflicting political elements. Such apparent contradictions are easily harmonized if the course of action results in the advance of the Communist cause. Soviet intelligence is not "above" channeling financial or other assistance to ultraconservative groups whose positions, however unwittingly, advance long-term Communist goals. Soviet and ultraconservative interests occasionally coincide, e.g., resistance to needed reforms and opposition to foreign business "encroachments." Moreover, the extremism of the radical right frequently has the effect of splitting anti-Communist forces, thus impeding coordinated and effective action against Communist subversion.

An objective analysis, designed to assess the danger of international communism and the effectiveness of its tactics in Latin America, meets with numerous obstacles. There are psychological problems which are in large part the purposeful creations of the Communists themselves. Communists have been successful in fashioning an image of strength, when in fact they are weak. They have created the impression that they have an ideology which is appealing, when in fact it is empty and worn. In heated debates they have encouraged black-and-white distinctions as to whether a given person or movement is Communist or non-Communist, whereas their tactics avoid such differentiation and exploit the operationally naïve who do not follow their devious path of opportunism. They have created fear when the reality calls for confidence within the West. They pose as reformers who constitute the vanguard of revolutionary change, whereas in reality they are reactionaries who make up a rear guard which is resisting the liberalizing influences of the West. The duplicity which is so much at the heart of Communist tactics has complicated not only the assessment of the strength of the Communist movement but also an understanding of its very nature.

The strength of communism in the Americas rests not so much on ideological foundations as on the deftness and finesse with which Moscow and Peking apply their operational and organizational techniques. While the electoral and numerical strength of the Latin American Communists is unimpressive, their psychological operations give the impression of strength and their political-action techniques provide them leverage in their campaign for seizing power.

What the Communists fear most of all is recognition of the conspiratorial nature of their movement and perception of their vulnerabilities. Balancing the variant North American and Latin American estimates of Communist strength in the Americas, available evidence supports the broad generalization that the Communists are much more dangerous than recognized by most Latin Americans, but much less powerful than assumed by most North Americans. These divergent estimates of the threat complicate effective inter-American action against Communist subversion in the Americas. The question of how much and what *kind* of effort is needed to thwart Communist advances is a major issue confronting the United States policy maker. Defensive measures against Communist subversion must be combined with positive programs to accelerate Latin American modernization and integration within the West. Thus, the policy issue is directly related to the question of relative priorities and allocation of United States resources.

8

The United States
Impact upon
Latin America's
Modernization

Long the object of Western dynamism, Latin America continues to absorb at a mounting rate the energizing impulses of the modern West. Western thought, organizational skill, and technology have effected a fundamental transformation of many areas of Latin America. The United States, through a variety of public and private activities, has made a major contribution to Latin American modernization. The magnitude of United States influence is best examined by reference to those public and private programs in Latin America which relate to the pursuit of one objective of a Strategy for the Americas, namely, the creation of a more closely integrated Western world in which Latin America is an active participant.

United States objectives in Latin America, while numerous in their specification, have three general and related purposes: first, to prevent the establishment within the Western Hemisphere of a hostile power capable of endangering the security of the Americas; second, to foster the development of an inter-American system effective in resolving regional issues and useful in coordinating political, economic, and other matters of mutual interest; third, to apply its public and private resources and skills to push Latin America's modernization through evolutionary and democratic means.

I. Defense of the Americas

United States military-strategic interests within the hemisphere have been the subject of previous comment.[1] The advancement of these interests requires both diplomatic action and military collaboration between the nations of the Americas. Before considering various approaches to hemispheric defense, the relevance of defense to Latin America's modernization process merits mention. A society under threat of attack—whether external or internal—must expend for purposes of defense resources that might otherwise be employed constructively for modernization. A country lacking internal stability does not attract foreign investment. Subversive elements obstruct those reforms which might reduce dissatisfaction. Military forces, which might otherwise be engaged in public projects for the satisfaction of socioeconomic needs, must be placed on military alert. In short, a society under siege must divert part of its attention from constructive programs in order to assure its mere survival.

Defense is needed against direct and overt extrahemispheric military attack and against indirect and covert subversion. Beyond this guardian role, military forces can serve as constructive instruments for socioeconomic change and development. These roles, while interrelated, are likely to receive a different stress from area to area, depending upon local circumstances.

As evidence of Soviet expansion mounted during the years following World War II, diplomatic efforts to obtain an inter-American agreement for hemispheric defense received the general support of Latin Americans. The Rio Treaty of 1947 had as its primary objective the building of an inter-American line of defense against extrahemispheric military attack. United States attention to the internal security needs of the relatively safe area of Latin America was minimal until 1957. The United States Military Assistance Program (USMAP) in Latin America

[1] See chap. 1.

during most of the 1950s consisted largely of efforts to strengthen the defense of the Panama Canal and assure continued access to hemispheric strategic materials. The general collaboration of the Latin American military was cultivated and standardization of equipment used by Latin America's armed forces was fostered. United States assistance usually took the form of transfers of military "hardware" through sales, loans, or grants.

The Communist efforts to seize Guatemala by subversion in 1954 posed a different kind of threat than that envisaged by the Rio Treaty of 1947. While Communist unconventional warfare was no less hostile to the interests of hemispheric security than the threat of overt military action, United States attempts on the diplomatic front to erect a system of multilateral defense against the indirect techniques of Communist subversion have achieved only limited success. The Inter-American Conference held at Caracas in 1954 took a positive but relatively ineffectual step toward developing a multilateral inter-American defense against indirect Communist conflict techniques. Many Latin Americans remained apprehensive lest United States action against Communist penetration be used as a cloak for "Yankee intervention." The failure of the Organization of American States to take earlier and stronger action against Castro's Cuba attests to the weakness of multilateral inter-American action whenever the Communist threat is not overt, direct, and patently extrahemispheric.

The United States revised its Military Assistance Program to meet needs which diplomatic efforts had failed to serve. The USMAP had drawn fire from critics who contended that Latin American military forces would have an unimportant role in a future world conflict. By 1959, however, with Castro's seizure of power, problems of internal security loomed large. Internal security could no longer be viewed simply as an adjunct to conventional hemispheric defense but as essential in combatting Communist-inspired "wars of national liberation."

The shift in emphasis from conventional military defense to internal security did not spare the USMAP from strong criticism. Some critics argued that, under the guise of internal security, the United States, through its military assistance, had propped up an assortment of dictatorial regimes. Other critics argued that even when United States military aid did not benefit authoritarian regimes, Latin American military forces supported ultraconservative civilians who—in their stubborn defense of the *status quo*—paid little heed to democratic processes or popular will. Ultraconservatism of this type, they alleged, was the *cause* of internal instability rather than the defense against it.[2]

United States military assistance *might* be used in some instances by would-be military *caudillos* or by ultraconservatives. This possibility must be considered as a calculated risk which the United States policy maker must weigh against the alternative of inaction in the face of internal subversion within friendly Latin American nations. The Communist-infiltrated Arbenz regime in Guatemala, the Castro take-over in Cuba, and the FALN (Fuerzas Armadas de la Liberación Nacional) campaign of terror in Venezuela give substance to the threat of internal subversion and provide justification for continuing United States measures to strengthen the counterinsurgency capability of Latin American armed forces.[3] Faced with these practical considerations, United States policy makers succeeded in obtaining increased support for the USMAP through the 1950s. Expenditures for the program grew from $200,000 in fiscal year 1952 to nearly $54 million in fiscal year 1959. The total United States military assistance commitment to Latin America throughout this period was approximately $317 million. The relatively low priority accorded the USMAP in Latin America is revealed by the fact that the last figure was less than 2 per cent of worldwide United States military assistance during the same period. USMAP expenditures in Latin America throughout the above period were about 5 per cent of what Latin American nations themselves have expended for military purposes. USMAP expenditures in Latin America increased rapidly through the early 1960s—obviously in reaction to the threat represented by Castro's Cuba—to

---

[2] For a critical commentary on United States military assistance to Latin America, see Edwin Lieuwen, *Arms and Politics in Latin America*, Praeger, New York, 1961. Senatorial criticism is reflected in the *Congressional Record*, Aug. 2, 1962, pp. 14409–14415, especially in the speech by Senator Gruening and comments by Senators Morse and Proxmire.

[3] Lieuwen, *op. cit.*, pp. 200–236.

reach a high point of $121,300,000 in fiscal year 1962. Expenditures for fiscal year 1964 and fiscal year 1966 were $68,900,000 and $77,300,000 (proposed), respectively.

Differences in the traditions of Latin America's military forces and the shifting social origins of its officer corps have led even some of the sharpest critics to concede that the Latin American military can be a positive force for change rather than a constant support of the *status quo*. The Latin American military has both opposed and defended authoritarian regimes. While they have frequently staged *golpes de estado* in defiance of civil authority, the Latin American military has on other occasions been called upon by civilian elements to intervene when civilian factionalism threatened anarchy.

Moreover, the Dominican crisis of April–June 1965 points to the need for an inter-American military force—under multilateral OAS command—prepared to take effective, immediate, and constructive action in the defense of the OAS system and the principles for which it stands. The eventual creation of such a force by the OAS late in May 1965, while intended to deal exclusively with the Dominican crisis, might well serve as a useful precedent to a more permanent establishment. The creation of a permanent inter-American military force could well be the most solid and constructive result of the anarchic conditions which prompted the United States intervention in the Dominican Republic.

Military intervention in political matters has by no means ceased. But the old stereotype of the military *caudillo* motivated by a lust for power and wedded to the interests of a narrow oligarchy no longer accurately describes the situation. As opposed to the roughshod power grabs of the nineteenth century, military juntas have at times been motivated by a desire to support forces for social and economic change. Moreover, the long-term trend—exceptions and occasional reverses to the contrary—appears to be toward civilian control of the military.[4]

The changing image of the Latin American military lends support to the current USMAP policy of favoring *civic-action* and *nation-building* programs which fit the developmental needs of

[4] Lieuwen, *op. cit.*, p. 171.

Latin America. Public works projects are required to open virgin territory. New transportation facilities must be built. Health and sanitation projects are needed. These and other proposals form part of a new approach that offers much promise. *If* indigenous or United States–stimulated civic-action or nation-building programs obtain the support of Latin America's military, a major United States policy problem may have been resolved. The *if* must be stressed, however, for not all Latin American military establishments will be easily convinced that they should forsake the acquisition of military "hardware" suitable for a combat role which is remote in reality. While retaining conventional military or internal security functions as needed, the Latin American military must now advance constructive and positive programs that will facilitate the integration of their nations into the modern West.

Civic action and nation building are not new to some of the military forces of Latin America. The armies of Argentina, Brazil, and Mexico have used this approach for some years. But now, under the impetus of the USMAP, more extensive programs are being encouraged and supported. The work of an outstanding Brazilian military unit illustrates the approach:

> The First Engineering Group of the Brazilian Army which carries out a program in five Northeastern states is even more closely identified with civilian interests than is the Brazilian Army as a whole. In addition to the normal responsibilities of a military unit—the First Group of Engineers constructs roads, dams, and irrigation works in the vast dry poligon area, and lends social assistance to its components and their families (including civilian laborers) as well as to the general population in regions where its projects are underway during periods of emergency, such as droughts or floods. The overall objective of the First Group is stated as that of integrating the Northeast into the national community.[5]

Venezuela has already launched a military civic-action program whose tasks include a tree-nursery system for building up forest industries, construction and repair of outlying roads, a

[5] United States Agency for International Development, *Northeast Survey Report*, Jan. 30, 1962, pp. 43–44.

geologic survey, and the training of army recruits in farm and livestock administration prior to their return to civilian life.

In the final analysis, the future of the USMAP in Latin America may depend upon the success or failure of civic action and nation building. In many Latin American countries the military forces represent both an important internal power factor and a skilled, disciplined group of men who could provide the impetus needed to speed desirable socioeconomic change. Some Latin American military establishments contain members of a new elite with whom the United States must work.

II. Building an Effective Inter-American System

United States national objectives are generally compatible with Latin American goals—at least to the degree that the latter include preservation of hemispheric peace, political stability, rapid economic growth, and social justice. In view of the compatibility between basic United States and Latin American goals, it would seem that an inter-American regional system such as the OAS should provide an effective instrument for hemispheric collaboration. But the OAS, though acting effectively on some matters, functions poorly on others. While the ineffectiveness of the OAS is often ascribed to administrative shortcomings, the fundamental difficulties are essentially psychological. Latin Americans harbor a residual fear of United States power, together with an envy of United States wealth. The very process of modernization itself frequently generates tensions. Naturally, Communist and other anti–United States elements foster resentments and exacerbate United States–Latin American relations. Feeble or tardy OAS responses to indirect and covert Communist infiltration stem in large part from psychological factors. Continued failure to reconcile Article 15 of the OAS Charter with contemporary world realities is a symptom. The lack of an OAS consensus on how to isolate more effectively Castro's Cuba, and confront with dispatch such emergencies as the Dominican crisis of April–June 1965, is a consequence. United States governmental efforts to counter the psychological barriers which impede inter-American harmony have been centered largely in the activities of the United States Information Agency (USIA).

USIA functions as a major United States transmitter of the "New Enlightenment" of the modern West. It attempts to counter the adverse psychological reactions which block inter-American harmony, to strengthen the cultural links between the Americas and to transfer the knowledge and techniques of the modern West and thus speed the modernization of Latin America.

USIA, known overseas as United States Information Service (USIS), is active in seven media: radio, TV, movies, press, book publishing, exhibits, and the arts. One of the most noteworthy of USIA's activities—the Binational Center Program—is conducted with the close collaboration and support of Latin American citizens. As of early 1965 USIS maintained 113 binational centers and binational societies throughout Latin America, teaching English to more than 177,000 Latin Americans annually. Other forms of cultural exchange are also carried out by these binational groups.

USIS posts administer educational and cultural exchanges between North Americans and Latin Americans conducted under the auspices of the Department of State. From 1949 through 1964 about 10,700 Latin Americans visited the United States under cultural exchange programs; of these more than 2,200 were students.[6] One special type of exchange, the foreign leader program, brings key personalities to the United States for a few weeks or months to familiarize them with American life and to visit those institutions, public or private, which are of special interest to them.

USIS libraries in Latin America, a major facet of this Agency's program, hold over 225,000 books. In some areas, USIS libraries are rated as the best available. In a closely related field, the distribution of books and pamphlets, USIA has been hampered in the past by budgetary limitations imposed by Congress. Increased Congressional appropriations, however, have added

* From 1944 through 1964 AID and its predecessor organizations sponsored the studies in the United States of over 21,000 Latin Americans.

funds for the USIA's book translation program for Latin America. Yet USIA's activity in this field is dwarfed by the efforts of Communist countries.

The short-wave broadcasts of the Voice of America (VOA) constitute an important part of USIA's program. It is indicative of United States failure to support adequately its Latin American information program that the VOA was silent in Latin America throughout most of the 1950s. USIA's Spanish language broadcasts were discontinued in 1953 and not restored until March 1960. As of 1964 they totaled 63 hours a week in Spanish and 23½ in Portuguese. VOA broadcasts to Latin America now utilize the world's largest and most powerful long-range transmitter. Although the VOA has gained a reputation for truthful presentation of the news, its impact in Latin America is difficult to judge. USIA's radio activity is not confined to VOA. A number of locally produced programs supplement the Agency's effort and may well surpass the VOA in overall impact. A combination effort utilizing VOA-taped programs distributed from Washington and placed with local Latin American standard wave broadcasting stations has been employed with good effect. Numerous Latin American radio stations rebroadcast taped VOA programs in whole or in part.

Television has made great strides in several Latin American countries in recent years, and USIA programming has been adjusted to this change with apparently good effect. It is anticipated that satellite communications systems will eventually provide a major communications breakthrough which USIA can exploit. USIA news releases funneled through press outlets form a major mass-impact effort to present to millions of Latin Americans the United States view on principal world issues. USIA's movie program has been less impressive. Some good documentaries and news "shorts" have been produced, but the program falls short of the need and the audience potential. Latin Americans are avid movie-goers, giving this medium an audience of many millions which includes illiterates who might not otherwise be reached by the USIA.

All in all, USIA programs of information and cultural exchange contain much that is commendable. Most defects can be traced to extra-agency causes. The United States is a novice in the field of foreign propaganda work and has had to acquire, rather than simply mobilize, experience in the many techniques involved. Moreover, despite highly developed domestic techniques in advertising and public relations, there has been a certain distrust in projecting a favorable United States image abroad. Herein lies a fundamental weakness of the USIA effort: the United States Congress has simply not been convinced that an expanded United States information and cultural-exchange program is worthy of support. Operating with a worldwide budget of $140 million in fiscal year 1966, USIA continued to be severely limited in developing its potential.

One of the problems USIA faces in convincing the Congress that its program deserves liberal support lies in the difficulty of demonstrating the effectiveness of its activities. As former USIA Director Edward R. Murrow has suggested:

> ... we cannot gauge our success by sales ... no cash register rings when a man changes his mind, no totals are rung up on people impressed with an idea ... often one's best work may be merely to introduce doubt into minds already firmly committed.[7]

The incongruity of an outpouring of United States largess in one direction and parsimony in another—when the two efforts are closely linked—is illustrated by comparing United States investment in the *Alianza* with that in USIA's Latin American program. The United States is committed to a $20 billion *Alianza* program which was launched with all the techniques of Madison Avenue. Yet one of the principal failures of the *Alianza* to date has been informational and psychological—a failure to communicate an understanding of the depth of Latin America's problems, a realization of the sacrifices and effort required to solve them, and a sense of popular participation in a joint undertaking. USIA's limited funds, however, cannot support the extensive informational program the *Alianza* needs.

USIA is simply scratching the surface in its present Latin American program. This is true in a very fundamental sense which transcends the above review of its current activities and

[7] *The New York Times,* Sept. 8, 1963.

budgetary problems. In fact, USIA does not have the charter to perform its part in the psychological struggle being waged in the contemporary conflict of systems. The battle for the minds of men requires not only the influencing of opinions but also the instilling of deeply felt *convictions* which will serve to identify Latin America with the dynamic values of the modern West. Some of USIA's programs no doubt achieve a measure of success in the latter and more profound type of psychological engineering. Yet one wonders whether its audience is not, for the most part, already favorably inclined. To the degree that this is not so, it may be asked whether the bland, hyperobjective, and detached characteristics of USIA's approach are sufficient to capture the minds and hearts of the uncommitted, much less the hostile. USIA has neither charter nor means to disseminate the propaganda which not only influences opinions but instills convictions. Nor has an alternative governmental program been undertaken to provide what could be a key instrument in *transmitting the human attitudes* which must underlie Latin America's development and integration into the modern West.

The United States private sector has contributed to giving Latin Americans a better understanding of life in the United States, as well as serving as a major channel for the infusion of the ideas, knowledge, and values of the modern West. United States films, for example, are the principal means of entertainment for the great mass of Latin American people. United States–produced movies account for approximately two-thirds of the film distribution in Latin America and an even larger percentage of foreign-film imports. Most of Latin America's imported TV programs are produced in the United States.

The United States publishing industry is a leading source for book imports in many Latin American countries. A growing demand for scientific and technological books is being met by United States publishers. United States periodicals also find a ready market in Latin America. The Spanish edition of *Time International* enjoys a circulation of over 95,000; that of *Life en Español* surpasses 425,000. Perhaps the most popular foreign periodical in all of Latin American is the *Reader's Digest*. The

Spanish edition of the *Reader's Digest* (entitled *Selecciones*) has a circulation of more than 1,300,000, and the Portuguese edition (*Seleções*) has a circulation of approximately 400,000. In addition, United States wire services supply Latin American news media with a good proportion of their coverage on international events.

The objective of building a stronger cultural bridge to link the Americas is one to which the United States private sector—as will be noted in greater detail subsequently—has contributed greatly. It must be added that the full potential of United States movie and TV producers and the United States publishing industry for serving as carriers of the New Enlightenment has by no means been fully tapped. A coordinated public-private effort in this field could vastly increase the United States impact on Latin America's modernization.

III. United States Public and Private Programs for Spurring Latin America's Development

United States efforts to strengthen hemispheric defense and build a more effective inter-American system—as important as they are in providing the stability and organizational framework for Latin American modernization—do not measure up in the popular mind as having nearly as much impact on Latin America's progress as those activities more closely related to accelerating economic growth through the flow of capital and trade.

The phrase "foreign aid" has been much used and much abused, just as the ill-defined term "development" has been both overworked and misunderstood. In the popular mind foreign aid is frequently equated with the transfer of *financial* resources just as development is very often equated with economic growth. Both aid and development, however, have a broader perspective. Aid includes not only capital transfers but also many forms of technical assistance. Similarly, development—viewed in its human as well as its material dimensions—requires political stability, investment in education, social change, and cultural transformation. In brief, there is a *human factor*—the changing of popular attitudes toward work, savings and investment—that must accompany the influx of capital if Latin America is to derive the maximum benefit from United States aid.

A qualitative analysis of United States governmental aid to Latin America is difficult because of differing criteria as to what programs properly constitute aid. Many export-import bank loans take the form of commercial transactions designed primarily to promote United States exports. The disposal of surplus United States agricultural products under Public Law 480—granted its beneficial results to the recipients—is motivated in large part by the desire to reduce storage costs or make way for new surpluses produced by a subsidized and highly efficient United States farming sector. On the other hand, when Latin Americans complain of adverse terms of trade and appeal for commodity-stabilization plans, they are requesting concessions that are inseparable from aid. To be sure, advantageous terms of trade represent a United States resource. The voluntary transfer of this resource, whether by commodity-stabilization agreements or other arrangements, represents a form of aid. Thus, aid and trade have become more and more inextricably linked.

Another common misconception concerning the function of foreign aid and the process of development is related to the capacity of a given country or region to make effective use of the credit or capital transfers frequently associated with an aid program. It is precisely this misunderstanding which has led many Latin Americans to compare the heavy flow of United States assistance to Western Europe under the Marshall Plan with a much smaller amount of assistance to Latin America and to conclude that the United States has neglected its hemispheric neighbors. The comparison fails to take account of the fact that Western Europe possessed in 1947—despite the ravages of World War II—vast administrative, entrepreneurial, and technical skills. Western Europe could absorb billions of dollars of Marshall Plan aid. In contrast, Latin America's ability to make effective use of financial and technical assistance is considerably more limited.

Fortunately there is increasing recognition of the fact that the development process requires far more than the simple transfer of capital and technical resources from country A to country B. Such a transfer represents an important factor in the development process, but it can hardly be expected to create a modern industrialized society where the many other prerequisites do not exist. *Latin America's development depends largely upon a cultural transformation which will produce those human attitudes that will support the dynamic social and economic institutions of the modern West.*

The Alliance for Progress

The Alliance for Progress, launched by President Kennedy in March 1961, provides the most dramatic example of a growing United States concern with the need to stimulate Latin America's development. The inter-American conference which produced the Charter of Punta del Este in August 1961 set forth the *Alianza's* goals. Since attainment of these objectives would represent a major socioeconomic transformation of Latin America, it is important to examine them in the light of the Latin American reality and of United States strategy for aid and development.

The Charter of Punta del Este restated political principles long held in high regard by the nations of the Americas. The Charter declares that the *Alianza's* goals of economic growth and social progress will be pursued "within the framework of personal dignity and political liberty." The principle of self-help is accepted as fundamental to the entire development process. The Charter also proclaims its fealty to democratic ideals of representative democracy and self-determination.

The objectives of the *Alianza* include greater economic integration among Latin American nations; reform of existing tax structures; creation of essential credit facilities with reasonable rates of interest; stimulation of private savings; encouragement of cooperative programs; consultative arrangements to consider marketing problems of Latin America's primary products; attraction of foreign investment; stimulation of domestic private enterprise in national development plans; integration into national development programs of the potential represented by local governments, decentralized agencies, and nongovernmental entities such as labor organizations, cooperatives, business and industrial groups; increased technical and professional training with emphasis on science and technology; more effective use of natural resources; more processing within Latin America of locally produced raw materials; full use of all communications media in an intensified effort to end the ignorance of the people of the Americas of each other and the conditions prevailing in their countries.

These principles and objectives constitute the positive aspects of the Alliance for Progress. They bespeak a dedication to those attitudes and techniques which have given the modern West its dynamism. Unfortunately the *Alianza* Charter also contains certain provisions, some of which are simply vague, and others of which are unrealistic in the goals they project. At times the Charter is silent on matters of crucial importance.

A recurrent theme of equalization appears in the Charter. It is said that less developed countries are to receive "maximum priority" in the distribution of *Alianza* resources as well as "special, fair, and equitable treatment" in the process of economic integration. A "leveling" approach is implicit. At another juncture, it is asserted that the benefits of economic progress must, as a fundamental *Alianza* goal, be made available to all citizens through "a more equitable distribution of national income." Sound tax policy, the Charter states, is that which contributes to "social progress through a more equitable distribution of income."

The practicality of such provisions must be questioned. It is difficult to imagine Brazil and Argentina, for example, granting priority attention to the needs of Paraguay and Bolivia, or pursuing effective measures designed to achieve a leveling in their own societies.

The awakened material aspirations of Latin America must be matched by increased *productivity*. The weighted emphasis on distributive rather than productive goals in the *Alianza* Charter—to the degree that it reflects a sincere inter-American consensus—is a matter of considerable concern, especially since the attainment of other Charter goals will place even greater demands on Latin America's productive resources. For example, the Charter calls for a variety of measures designed to provide better sanitation, nutrition, and health. Granting the humanitarian motive behind such goals, there is some question as to whether they merit priority action *unless and until* increases in productivity provide the economic resources for greater welfare measures. Should Latin America's productivity fail to rise sharply, social improvements may simply be negated by continued impoverishment and social ferment. Lincoln Gordon, the United States Ambassador to Brazil, has suggested that what is needed is for

> . . . all elements in the community to expand productivity rather than a self-defeating effort to equalize poverty . . . [and] the basic philosophy is to promote rapid economic development in order to increase total production—the total availability of goods and services—simultaneously providing for their more equitable distribution for the full participation in progress by all segments of the population. Without much greater total output, mere redistribution of incomes would simply mean distributing poverty.[8]

The problem of achieving the proper balance between economic investment for productive purposes and investment for social improvements is complex. While *some* social investments have a distributive flavor and may be motivated more by political demagoguery than by any other consideration, *other* forms of social investment can contribute directly to economic growth and productivity. Economic and social investments need not be mutually exclusive. Increasingly, expenditures for education are considered as investment rather than consumption. Put another way, expenditures in human capital—improved knowledge and skills of the populace—can be a highly productive form of investment and a direct contribution to economic growth.[9] As the

[8] Lincoln Gordon, *A New Deal for Latin America,* Harvard University Press, Cambridge Mass., 1963, pp. 53, 83.

[9] *Ibid.,* p. 70. In the United States, according to Lincoln Gordon, "recent evidence suggests that perhaps one-half of the four-fold increase in our per capita incomes during the last seventy-five years is due to the improvement in human capital through education and training. . . ." The development of human capital is a point on which the economist, sociologist and anthropologist join in focusing on the all-important *human factor.* For other discussions of this point see Theodore W. Schultz, "Investment in Human Capital,"

economist Raymond F. Mikesell has aptly put it, "development is basically a matter of changing the hearts and minds and capabilities of people." [10]

The Punta del Este Charter's emphasis on human-capital development is well placed. Some of the announced goals for broadening the educational structure, however, appear overly optimistic. It is doubtful whether the goal of eliminating adult illiteracy in Latin America by 1970 is realistic. The goal of assuring each school-age child a minimum of six years of primary education by 1970 will probably be impossible to attain. Such an achievement would increase primary school registration, according to the Charter itself, from approximately twenty-six million in 1960 to some forty-five million in 1970. The Charter's emphasis on eliminating illiteracy and magnifying primary school registration has in itself become open to question. There is growing recognition that, if Latin America is to produce the technical, managerial, and administrative talent it so clearly needs, greater emphasis must be placed on secondary and university education. Given the limited resources of Latin America, increasing the productive capacity of those who have already completed primary education may merit greater priority, since it is the skills of the latter that can be used to create the resources necessary to support more extensive primary programs. This, in essence, was the principal conclusion reached by an *Alianza*-sponsored conference of educators who met in Bogotá in August 1963.

Not only do these and certain other goals of the *Alianza* appear highly optimistic and needlessly explicit, but they suggest another *caveat* lest expectations be unduly stimulated. Latin America's social structure must be sufficiently flexible and its economy sufficiently dynamic to utilize the skills and knowledge

---

American Economic Review, March 1961, pp. 1–17. Also Theodore W. Schultz, *The Economic Test in Latin America,* Bulletin 35, New York State School of Industrial and Labor Relations, Cornell University, Ithaca, N.Y., 1956, pp. 17–20.

[10] United States Senate, Subcommittee on American Republics Affairs of the Committee on Foreign Relations, *United States–Latin American Relations— Some Observations on the Operation of the Alliance for Progress: The First Six Months,* 87th Cong., 2d Sess., 1962, p. 13.

of those who reap the advantages of an expanded and improved educational structure. Otherwise much of the investment in human capital will not only be wasted but may produce a growing crop of malcontents who will foster instability rather than progress. This is not to argue against any existing program for expanded educational opportunities but simply to emphasize that Latin American development must progress along a broad front.

With respect to certain important problems the Charter is silent. It shows no recognition of the population explosion, a basic factor affecting Latin American socioeconomic development.[11] In fact, as indicated above, some social investments will aggravate this problem. Nor does the Charter specify the course to be followed in developing industrial power resources, long in short supply in Latin America and a prerequisite for economic diversification and industrialization. Perhaps the Charter's reference to "more efficient use of natural resources" was intended to cover this factor in a few words, but it would appear to deserve more attention in plans for Latin America's modernization than it received at Punta del Este.

The Charter is replete with references to price fluctuations for primary products. It reflects here and there grave concern lest restrictive measures adopted by the European Common Market aggravate this problem. Nowhere does the Charter shed its defensive tone on this issue in favor of a *positive* proposal for joint consultation and action within a broadened Western Community. This area of silence is disconcerting, since it encompasses so many points that are crucial to generating the dynamism required for Latin America's rapid advance.

In the operation of the *Alianza* much reliance is placed on the development of rationally integrated national plans to establish mutually consistent targets, assign priorities, and channel investment. Commitments of internal resources and pledges of reforms constitute part of the planning process. As an instrumentality, national planning in Latin America appears essential, given the cultural values, traditional institutions, limited resources, soaring

[11] In practice some *Alianza* funds have been directed recently toward population-control measures.

population, and rising material aspirations. Latin Americans, if they are to resolve the formidable problems facing them, must coordinate their activities and set priorities. These tasks demand a higher degree of state initiative than North Americans are accustomed to accept as necessary or desirable. As an instrumentality, national planning per se need not nullify the political liberties and private economic initiative of a free society. If guided by authoritarian minds and a statist philosophy, however, national planning could lead to the suppression of human freedom and the stifling of private initiative.

The Latin American planner is generally eclectic in his economic philosophy, but at the same time he may frequently find it difficult to move from his planning board to practical field administration. Although accustomed to certain authoritarian and statist forms, he resists offense against his personal dignity or restriction of the reasonably free play of his individualistic spirit. Such a combination leads to the hope that Latin America's form of national planning will stimulate rather than impede private initiative and support the dynamic market system of the modern mixed economy.

Latin America has an abundance of economic dogma. More than anything else, Latin America needs the human attitudes and institutions conducive to modernization. To the degree that planning organizations respect the political principles of Punta del Este and contribute toward the growth of economic productivity, they deserve support. To the degree that Latin American planning organizations do not serve these ends, they have no place in the *Alianza* program and do not merit United States encouragement.

In the final analysis, the success of national planning in the Alliance for Progress program may depend upon the ability of Latin Americans to harness the potential of the private economic sector, both domestic and foreign. Approximately $70 billion of the *Alianza's* ten-year investment is expected to come from foreign and domestic private investors. Despite the preponderant role envisioned for the private sector, however, the *Alianza* has operated to date largely on a government-to-government basis. United States private investments have fallen short of the investment goals established at Punta del Este. For a program that relies as heavily as does the *Alianza* on the participation of United States and Latin American private sectors (70 per cent of the total commitment), the ascertainable record to date does not suggest the likelihood that the *Alianza* will attain its investment goals unless vigorous and effective action is taken to stimulate greater private participation.

Alianza progress has been a matter of considerable debate. Much time has been required to construct its administrative machinery. Latin Americans have accused the United States of unwarranted bureaucratic delays. The United States has lamented Latin American reluctance to undertake necessary reforms and inertia in formulating feasible national plans. Nevertheless, *Alianza* reports describe a variety of positive steps which have begun to inject momentum into the program. Colombia, Chile, Bolivia, Venezuela, Mexico, Ecuador, Peru, Honduras, and Panama have presented development plans. Several countries have started to institute tax reforms and boost agrarian productivity. A number of homes, classrooms, water systems, medical centers, and roads have been constructed. Yet when *Alianza* progress is balanced against the soaring population and the vast needs of Latin America, the scope of untouched tasks dwarfs the accomplishments. A widespread feeling persists that inordinate delays and waning enthusiasm have stalled the *Alianza* program.

Part of the *Alianza's* problem has been organizational. It has lacked a functioning command center, and direction of the program has been dispersed. Drs. Alberto Lleras Camargo and Juscelino Kubitschek (formerly Presidents of Colombia and Brazil, respectively) filed reports in June 1963 which confirmed this defect and recommended the creation of an Inter-American Development Committee. The organization which has been created in response to those reports—the Inter-American Committee for the Alliance for Progress or, as abbreviated in Spanish, CIAP —may enhance the spirit of joint enterprise and counter the prevalent tendency to regard the *Alianza* as "just another United States aid program." Miracles should not be expected from organizational innovations such as CIAP. As Lleras Camargo has declared:

The weaknesses of the Alliance for Progress and its consequent slowness or lack of active implementation are due mainly to political elements that it is impossible to correct with a minimum of structural changes. It is a mistake to believe that policies can be changed through organization; organization does whatever the governments want it to do.[12]

It is too early to estimate the degree of success which the *Alianza* may achieve. In 1962 and 1963 the increase in per capita domestic product ranged between 0.6 and 1 per cent—a drop from 1961 levels, and well short of the *Alianza* goal of 2.5 per cent annually. Ten of the nineteen Latin American countries exceeded the 2.5 per cent *Alianza* goal during the period; however, overall performance was retarded by the economic crises in Argentina and Brazil. Finally, in 1964, Latin America as a whole registered its first breakthrough of the 2.5 per cent *Alianza* target: an encouraging 5.5 per cent overall average (offset by a 3 per cent increase in the region's population). Performance in 1965 is expected to exceed the 2.5 per cent target figure.

The GNP measuring stick has many obvious shortcomings. Its use by *Alianza* officials themselves—as evidenced by the statistics cited above—is probably prompted by the explicit and much-publicized *Alianza* goal of attaining an average growth rate of 2.5 per cent per annum. But obviously GNP figures will be influenced by adverse factors (natural disasters, political instability, unfavorable world commodity markets, and so on) over which the *Alianza* program can exercise no control. Conversely, rapid GNP advances due to unusually favorable world commodity market conditions cannot be cited as evidence of the *Alianza's* success. It is sufficient to say that the *Alianza* contains many positive features, has made advances in developing sound economic planning procedures, and has improved its organizational machinery. In the final analysis, until and unless a better program can be devised

[12] The Lleras Camargo and Kubitschek reports are published by the Pan American Union and identified respectively as Documents C-d-1103 and C-d-1102, both issued on June 15, 1963. The reports differed markedly in tone and diagnosis, although in essential agreement on the *Alianza's* organizational defects and the need for creating an Inter-American Development Committee.

—and there is no evidence of one on the horizon—the *Alianza* represents the major inter-American effort to spur Latin America's economic growth during the decade of the 1960s.

Constructive criticism of the *Alianza* has induced needed corrections. But destructive criticism, largely based on ignorance of the immensity of the challenge, has served to sow confusion and defeatism. The Alliance for Progress cannot effect sweeping and immediate changes in Latin America. It would be fallacious to assume that economic growth and social progress, prime goals of the *Alianza*, automatically lead to political freedom and inter-American harmony. The modern West did not develop its human resources or make its technological breakthroughs overnight, and it would be unrealistic to expect a better performance of Latin America. The *Alianza* offers no panacea for the complex problems confronting this region. Effective political leadership must stress the positive points of the *Alianza* and deemphasize its equivocal and less realistic aspects. The *Alianza* can be vitalized through a dynamic and imaginative program of political action. As in all things, *the leadership of men of action is required*.[13]

The Peace Corps

As of early 1965 approximately 10,500 volunteers were enrolled in the Peace Corps, with about 40 per cent of the total in Latin America. Volunteers were assigned to rural and urban community-development projects, agricultural extension work, health projects, the formation of cooperatives, and a wide variety of educational programs. Agricultural extension work drew upon the services of 359 volunteers, while 280 were committed to health projects and 363 to educational programs of a wide variety.

The Peace Corps program in Latin America is much too young to permit more than an interim judgment, but it can be said that Peace Corps volunteers, working in backward areas, have had a wholesome effect. Their example contrasts favorably with the widespread impression that most Americans abroad, in official or

[13] Latin America's leadership problem was discussed in chap. 4.

private capacity, tend to congregate in a North American enclave and have limited contact with the local inhabitants.

The enthusiastic response to Peace Corps programs in Latin America is indicated by the fact that host countries have asked for additional volunteers. As early as 1954 El Salvador had established Social Progress Brigades which carried out activities similar to those of the Peace Corps. With the assistance of the International Secretariat for Volunteers Service, AID, and the United States Peace Corps, El Salvador had, by the end of 1964, organized seventeen "brigades" (usually of four persons each), composed of both United States Peace Corps and Salvadoran volunteers. The Argentine government is studying a proposal to send teachers to other Latin American countries as long-term volunteers. A Jamaican Youth Corps has operated two camps for boys between the ages of fifteen and nineteen since 1958 and has recently been considering the formation of a National Volunteer Corps for teaching and community development work in isolated areas. In October 1963 the Peruvian government organized the Cooperación Popular Universitaria with the objective of sending college students to aid rural community development during the summer vacation; over 540 students participated in the program during its first year of operation and about 1,200 had volunteered early in 1965. In addition to these government-sponsored programs, a variety of private activities have been launched by organizations in Bolivia, Chile, and Venezuela; a private group, similarly oriented, is in the planning stage in Ecuador. In short, the Peace Corps approach seems to have inspired some enthusiasm within Latin America for similar programs, with or without United States Peace Corps participation and support.

The Peace Corps is essentially a catalytic effort designed to stimulate self-help and community initiative in Latin America. The potentialities of the Peace Corps should not be overestimated. Solution of the deep and numerous problems of Latin America is not within the limited reach of Peace Corps volunteers. It is difficult to inspire the Latin American technician to get into the field and get his hands dirty by engaging in projects similar to those undertaken by the United States Peace Corpsman. Even the qualified and competent Latin American technician, true to his Iberian heritage, often feels it demeaning to apply in a practical way the knowledge he possesses. Peace Corps volunteers can expect to experience many frustrations as a result of these and other attitudes deeply rooted in the Iberian cultural tradition. Ultimately, the Peace Corps in Latin America must be judged not so much by its direct and immediate contribution as by the degree to which it inspires similar self-help programs by *Latin Americans themselves.*

Impact of the United States Private Sector on Latin America's Development

The activities of United States business enterprises, labor groups, academic institutions, private foundations as well as a wide assortment of religious and nonsectarian volunteer organizations have contributed in many ways to Latin America's development. While the details of these varied activities need not concern us here, the magnitude and impact of their contribution to Latin America's modernization is of interest. Over recent decades, the United States private sector has exerted a truly revolutionary force in Latin America. It has placed more personnel in the field, invested more resources, and spread its influence more widely than all public programs combined. In addition, a number of United States government efforts have depended upon the direct support of one or another element of the private sector.

United States Business

Enterprising Yankees made important contributions to the development of Latin America long before United States citizens had sizable capital investments there. As early as the 1840s, North American engineers, technicians, and entrepreneurs left their mark on Latin America.

> Citizens of the United States established Brazil's first geological survey, set up Argentina's first meteorological service, and helped President Sarmiento lay the foundations for Argentina's admirable system of public education. Hundreds of individual Americans also contributed to the progress of the area. Thus, a

Baltimore mechanic built sawmills, sugar mills, and flour mills in Ecuador; a typesetter from Philadelphia helped found *El Mercurio,* Chile's greatest newspaper; a Vermont Yankee introduced the first steam engines into Paraguay; and an unreconstructed rebel from Virginia became one of the world's greatest authorities on the mighty streams which form the system of the River Plate.[14]

United States entrepreneurs such as William Wheelwright, Henry Meiggs, Minor C. Keith, Percival Farqhuar, and the Harman Brothers sparked developments in Latin American transportation, mining, and manufacturing.

The application of the principle of mass production in the exploitation of low-grade Latin American ores brings to mind the names of Braden, Guggenheim, Kennecott, and Anaconda, American Smelting, and Cerro de Pasco. Bethlehem and United States Steel have proven the feasibility of utilizing remote deposits of iron ore. The agricultural development of lowland tropical areas owes a unique debt to the United Fruit Company. The practicability of large-scale enterprises has been shown by such firms as Goodrich, Chrysler, Westinghouse, and Kaiser. Merchandising methods have been profoundly influenced by Sears, Roebuck and Woolworth. Industrial productivity has been promoted by an assortment of United States business companies working in such diverse fields of activity as those suggested by such firms as United Shoe and Machinery, Singer, International Harvester, John Deere, General Electric, Ford, and General Motors. The introduction of office and busines machines has resulted from the aggressive distributing efforts of Remington, National Cash Register, and International Business Machines. The activities of W. R. Grace, as well as other United States entrepreneurs, demonstrate the benefits to be derived from highly diversified enterprises under a single management. The above list could be extended considerably. But the point is clear: United States private business has injected into Latin America an enormous amount

[14] Merwin L. Bohan, "United States Public and Private Investments in Latin America," *Proceedings of the Institute on Private Investment Abroad,* Southwestern Legal Foundation, 1962, p. 27.

of technological know-how, organizational skill, and entrepreneurial spirit which has contributed greatly to the area's modernization.

Many United States business organizations brought to Latin America skills acquired through years of experience, together with the knowledge which flows from continuing and sizable expenditures for research and development conducted in the United States. North American companies provide products and services that often set the pace for Latin American industries and thereby introduce healthy competition which benefits the Latin American consumer. United States manufacturing firms established in Latin America reduce dependence upon imports. Of Latin American export sales 30 per cent is the result of United States enterprise, which also provides, on an area-wide average, 15 per cent of the governmental revenues. United States companies have introduced advanced employer-employee practices. Comparatively high wages with generous benefits are characteristic of United States enterprise in Latin America. Technical training programs, generally combined with opportunities for advancement, enable Latin American employees to acquire valuable skills and attain top managerial positions. Less than 2 per cent of the employees in North American firms operating in Latin America are United States citizens. Undoubtedly this percentage will be reduced as Latin Americans in greater numbers acquire the skills necessary for managerial jobs.

Some measure of the magnitude of the impact of United States private business on Latin America can be obtained from the trade and investment statistics previously cited. The very fact that direct investments of United States private capital in Latin America totaled $10.3 billion as of early 1965, and comprised approximately 70 per cent of all foreign private investments, provides some gauge of the impact of United States business.[15] Statistics, of course, cannot begin to measure the importance of the many per-

[15] Petroleum development has attracted far more United States capital than any other activity. Manufacturing and mining-smelting activities rank second and third respectively. United States investments are heaviest in Venezuela, Brazil, Mexico, and Chile, in that order.

sonal contacts or the exchange of ideas that inevitably takes place as a result of a volume of commercial contacts between the United States and Latin America.

To be sure, United States business operations in Latin America have not been uniformly enlightened. Some United States companies have been accused of seeking special treatment, or wielding an unfair competitive advantage over their Latin American counterparts. United States businessmen have been criticized for living in enclaves and showing little concern for local culture and traditional business practices. The erratic flow of United States investments has been cited as an obstacle to the development planning of host countries. Many of these charges can be countered, particularly since they usually fail to recognize that United States corporate practices in Latin America have undergone considerable change since the early decades of the twentieth century.

United States businesses operating in Latin America are vulnerable to the psychological whiplash of a society which is experiencing profound cultural changes. Since United States business is itself one of the contributors to this transformation, it cannot but expect to bear the brunt of some of the inevitable reactions to its influence. It can be anticipated that Latin American governments will frequently restrict foreign enterprises from certain fields of activity and, in some cases, attempt to divert foreign resources into sectors considered to be in their national interest. Latin American entrepreneurs will generally exert pressure to channel foreign capital into joint ventures and noncompeting activities. Moreover, there can be no doubt but that ultranationalists, Leftists, Yankeephobes and Communist agitators will attempt to exploit all sources of tension between United States business organizations and their host countries.

The modernizing impulses transmitted to Latin America by United States business organizations, therefore, confront some important barriers. United States private investment in the area has declined sharply during the early 1960s. The nationalization of some private United States holdings, the uncompensated seizure of approximately $1 billion in United States private property in Castro's Cuba, and the fiscal policies followed by some Latin

American nations have all combined to dampen the interest of the private investors.

Strong measures are required to assure that the potential of United States private enterprise is fully harnessed to Latin America's development. Many of these measures depend upon United States private business initiative. There are oustanding examples to indicate that some United States companies have adopted enlightened programs which serve not only the interests of United States enterprise but also speed Latin America's modernization. To cite three of many possible examples, the activities of the Business Council for International Understanding (BCIU), the International Basic Economy Corporation (IBEC), and the Creole Investment Corporation illustrate the type of business initiative needed to bolster the image of United States private enterprise in Latin America.

The BCIU, supported by a number of United States enterprises including many with extensive operations in Latin America, provides executive business personnel with area-orientation courses designed to enhance their representative capabilities abroad. These courses are intended to instill a greater sense of cultural empathy; help the business executive represent the United States position on matters often misunderstood or misinterpreted abroad; create a better awareness of the methods, strength, and appeals of communism and other hostile ideologies in developing nations; and improve foreign-language abilities.

IBEC (an affiliate of the Rockefeller interests) has many characteristics of a private foundation, although its investments are intended to be profitable. Launched with the conviction that United States business could best stimulate the economies of less developed countries by initiating projects which are "generally a little too bold or too difficult for local investors," IBEC's imaginative leadership has brought substantial change to many Latin American countries. IBEC has invested in such diverse activities as food processing, supermarkets, modern dairy industries, hybrid-corn producers, scientific poultry farms, low-cost housing projects, and mutual funds for steering savings into productive use.

The Creole Investment Corporation, a subsidiary of Creole

Petroleum, began operations in September 1961 with $10 million in capital. Its objective is to invest in Venezuelan businesses unrelated to the parent company's oil interests. By May 1965 the Creole Investment Corporation had received over 400 proposals and had invested $7.33 million in twenty-four companies. These investments, made by subscribing as a minority stockholder, have been limited thus far to manufacturing, agriculture, and animal husbandry. Creole assigns one or two men to each associated company's board of directors. All earnings are to be reinvested as new opportunities arise. Other capital sources have supplied an estimated $21 million in response to Creole's leadership, indicating that local Latin American capital can be attracted to productive enterprises which show signs of success. Creole's reputation for managerial skill has supplied that needed element of confidence. Encouraged by Creole's accomplishments, the International Petroleum Company has plans for launching a similar venture in Colombia.

Enlightened programs such as those undertaken by BCIU, IBEC, and Creole must be supplemented by energetic United States business efforts along four principal lines: [16]

1. Merge more fully United States enterprises operating in Latin America into the fabric of the area's domestic economies.

2. Support United States tariff and quota changes which will grant increased access to the United States market for low-cost Latin American producers of petroleum, minerals, sugar, and certain types of semimanufactured articles.

3. Initiate a vigorous information campaign which will go beyond the limited purview of public relations and correct Marxian-inspired distortions of modern capitalism by building a more appealing image of the dynamic economies of the modern West.

4. Develop a closer coordination with United States public authorities so that private business interests in Latin Amer-

---

[16] Some of the points which follow will be the subject of additional comment in chap. 9.

ica can be protected with a minimum reliance upon the United States taxpayers' support of "all-risk guarantees" and "special tax advantages."

United States private enterprise in Latin America—in its own uncoordinated and yet effective way—has acted as one of the principal carriers of the dynamic human attitudes and techniques of the modern West. Much more is expected of it in *Alianza* planning, and it undoubtedly possesses a great potential that has yet to be fully tapped for modernizing Latin America.

There are encouraging signs which indicate a more active and coordinated response on the part of United States business to the challenge represented by Latin America. An International Executive's Service Corps (IESC)—frequently referred to as the "businessman's peace corps"—was established in June 1964. The IESC plans to send United States business executives to developing areas—including but not limited to Latin America. These executives, active or retired, will be selected from volunteers who have skills in production, finance, or marketing. They will be sent to advise foreign private enterprises which request and qualify for IESC assistance. Another promising step was taken in February 1965 with the creation of the Council for Latin America. The new organization, with 175 United States corporate members, merges the functions of the former Business Group for Latin America, the United States Inter-American Council and the Latin American Information Committee. The Council will work for closer public-private coordination, both in the United States as well as with Latin American contacts, in support of the Alliance for Progress.

United States Labor

Only since World War II has United States organized labor exerted an important impact upon Latin America. The fact that the Latin American regional labor organization, the *Confederación de Trabajadores de América Latina* (CTAL), had fallen under Communist domination in the mid-1940s aroused the concern of United States labor leaders. Non-Communist elements of the CTAL eventually split off from that organization in 1948 and founded an inter-American labor confederation which evolved into the *Organización Regional Interamericana de Trabajadores* (ORIT). Founded in Mexico City in 1951, ORIT has assumed leadership of the democratically oriented labor movement in Latin America. ORIT's success is underlined by the demise of the Communist-dominated CTAL in 1962. Communist-dominated labor conferences held in Santiago in late 1962 and in Brasilia in early 1964 failed to create a successor organization to the CTAL, further emphasizing the influence which ORIT has been able to exercise in countering Communist infiltration of Latin American labor. United States labor organizations deserve much of the credit for ORIT's successes.

In terms of personnel and material resources, United States labor's commitment in Latin America is relatively small when compared to that of United States business. Yet Latin America's development will be greatly aided if its labor organizations press for their legitimate rights, exercise their power with responsibility, develop the sophistication to discern and reject the blandishments of political demagogues, and avoid the incitement of extremist agitators. The American Federation of Labor–Congress of Industrial Organizations (AFL-CIO) has supported ORIT chiefly through leadership training, financial assistance, and technical advice. Similar support has been rendered through the International Trade Secretariats (ITS), many of which have also conducted effective action to counter Communist penetration within Latin America.

In more recent years, the United States labor movement has concentrated much of its efforts on supporting the activities of the American Institute for Free Labor Development (AIFLD), which has its headquarters in Washington, D.C. The AIFLD has many unique features. It is supported by AID and United States business organizations as well as by the AFL-CIO. Its social action programs are financed entirely by government funds channeled through AID. Thus, the AIFLD has become a focal point for United States action in support of a democratic Latin American labor movement. The AIFLD carries out a number of training programs throughout Latin America and supplements this activity by training selected Latin American labor leaders in the United States. Trainees return prepared to engage in organizational activity financed by the AIFLD. The AIFLD has also established housing projects—notably in Mexico and Honduras—designed to meet the needs of Latin American labor and has been active in creating credit unions and cooperatives.

The direct participation of United States labor in the defense of a democratic Latin American labor movement is illustrated by the role which it played in the early 1960s in the Dominican Republic and British Guiana. In the former nation, a bitter struggle prevented the newly organized labor unions (which had never been permitted during Trujillo's regime) from falling into the hands of Communist labor organizers. In British Guiana, the AFL-CIO, supported by ITS organizations and graduates of AIFLD training programs, rallied to the defense of democratic labor leaders and stymied the attempts of Cheddi Jagan to capture and place the labor movement in British Guiana under Communist control. The same democratic forces no doubt contributed to Cheddi Jagan's defeat in British Guiana's election of December 1964.

The activities of United States labor—unlike the more diffused influences of United States business and other private-sector undertakings—are concentrated in but one segment of Latin America's society. Nevertheless, labor is exercising an important influence in maintaining the type of stability upon which the socioeconomic changes required for Latin America's modernization must be based.

Other Private United States Efforts

A key element in Latin America's modernization is the development of its human resources. A number of United States private organizations have devoted their efforts to fulfilling this need while also supplying organizational and other techniques designed to increase Latin America's productivity. These diverse organizations include university groups, private volunteer organizations, religious associations, and private foundations. Since there is considerable overlap in their approaches, and they engage in a number of joint activities, it is appropriate to examine their combined efforts as a whole. In fact, it is in the totality of their efforts that their important role in promoting the United States objective of spurring Latin America's modernization becomes more clearly evident.

Latin American development has been retarded by an Iberian cultural-value pattern which resists change and has displayed an inadequate sense of mutual accommodation. Many private United States efforts have addressed themselves to this problem and have fostered community-development projects which, in many ways, are similar to some sponsored by the Peace Corps. A Cornell University project among the Quechua Indians of Vicos, Peru, focused on developing community cooperation and the application of new farming techniques. A traditional *hacienda* with its usual *patrón-peón* relationship and subsistence-level economy was transformed over a period of years into a self-respecting group of individual landowners. Increased agrarian productivity and greatly improved educational facilities were important features of the community-action program which produced Vicos' modernization. Effective community-action projects with a stress on self-help were also initiated by Acción, a private United States volunteer group which has done laudable work in the slums of Caracas. The introduction of new agrarian techniques and methods of constructing low-cost dwellings have been the focal points of other projects of community action undertaken by private United States organizations. In a related effort, Cooperative for American Relief Everywhere (CARE) has provided a variety of self-help kits, as well as tools and machines needed for community-development projects. CARE also has extended technical advice for these projects and has worked in close cooperation with Peace Corps volunteers in Colombia. Private United States groups have also helped to overcome another major weakness of Latin America's economy: lack of adequate capital formation. Credit unions established in Peru by a United States Maryknoll missionary, Father Dan McClellan, have achieved spectacular success and have been supplemented by related programs to provide needed low-cost housing.

These approaches have in common an important principle:

the value of extending assistance which encourages self-help measures that permit the individual to keep his pride while solving his problems on a community level. The importance of this principle was well stated by a CARE administrator who said, "it is not charitable to satisfy a man's hunger if, at the same time, you are undermining his self-respect." [17]

The multifaceted approach of private foundations represents a major segment of private United States activities in Latin America. During the three years from 1960 to 1962 the Ford, Kellogg, and Rockefeller Foundations granted over $25 million to Latin America; more than 100 other foundations, including Carnegie, Doherty, and W. R. Grace, added several millions more to this sum. Operating with great selectivity, the financial resources of these foundations have many times produced an important multiplier effect in disseminating the ideas of the modern West. From 1913 through 1964 the Rockefeller Foundation granted more than $80 million to Latin America for a great variety of purposes, e.g., improving agricultural techniques, public health, and medical education. The Kellogg Foundation has provided training in the United States for Latin American physicians, dentists, and nurses; it has also backed agricultural extension and research. The Ford Foundation has supported the creation of new skills for stimulating socioeconomic change and development and has extended grants for studies in the basic sciences, engineering, agronomy, economics, and teacher training. Some of the above foundations, as well as other private groups, have sponsored important university-to-university exchanges that have provided an opportunity for both students and professors to exchange knowledge and experience in many fields.

Reflecting upon the many activities of the United States private sector in Latin America—business, labor, volunteer groups of many types, foundations, and academic institutions—one must conclude that their combined impact is nothing short of revolutionary in the sense of providing an impetus for rapid change in fundamental aspects of Latin American life.

[17] David Luria, "Food for Progress," CARE release, January 1963, p. 7. (Mimeographed.)

Conclusion

United States public and private activities have made an impressive contribution to Latin America's modernization. Modern attitudes, organizational skills, and technology are being transmitted to Latin America through innumerable channels. United States public policies, viewed as a whole, appear to be in harmony with basic Latin American goals—at least to the extent that the latter can be defined as the preservation of hemispheric peace and the achievement of greater political stability along with rapid economic growth and social justice. Since such common goals are clearly consonant with the process of modernization, United States public policies and programs appear also to be serving a central United States strategic objective: the closer integration of Latin America within the modern West. The United States private sector, in turn, is making a major contribution to increasing Latin America's productivity in ways which enable its transitional societies to meet the growing aspirations of its people.

Both the United States public and private sectors have exhibited shortcomings in their approaches to Latin America. The United States has been burdened by a legacy of sporadic interest in the region. Spurts of intense concern with Latin American affairs have alternated with periods of indifference. The United States has frequently taken a defensive attitude toward the currents of change in Latin America. On the governmental side, *ad hoc* improvisations and reactive measures have given many United States policies a piecemeal and cautious appearance. Such policies hardly constitute a strategy for an area experiencing profound and rapid change. Furthermore, United States policies sometimes exhibit few signs of continuity and even less evidence of the United States policy makers' ability to anticipate events. In the private sector, United States business representatives have not always displayed that degree of cultural empathy which might have blunted many of the Latin American criticisms to which they have been subjected. Other United States businessmen are too often unmindful of the obvious need for collaborating more closely with their own government. Other segments of the private sector, though individually performing noteworthy services, can be criticized only insofar as their efforts have not been coordinated so as to achieve maximum effect. As a general commentary, *the lack of an integrated public-private response stands out as a major shortcoming of the United States approach to Latin America.*

Despite obvious inadequacies in the conduct of United States public and private activities in Latin America, United States efforts—on balance—have been basically sound. Many criticisms appear more valid when addressed to past attitudes and approaches rather than to those now current. Yet Latin America remains a major problem area to the United States policy maker. It would appear that United States responses to the challenge presented by Latin America, however positive and constructive they may be judged to be, have been inadequate in some important respects. Why has this been so?

Could it be that the magnitude of United States public and private efforts has been insufficient in view of the immense challenge posed by Latin America's quest for modernization? There is evidence to support such a conclusion, particularly when United States activities there are measured in monetary terms. The total United States public-private financial commitment to Latin America (including grants, loans, investments, reinvestments, private philanthropy, etc.) is not impressive when expressed as a percentage of the United States gross national product. Admitting the lack of accurate data to support a monetary measurement of this type, let us assume that United States public-private expenditures in Latin America total $3 billion annually. While this estimate probably exceeds the actual United States financial commitment, it represents less than one-half of 1 per cent of the United States GNP in 1964. Thus, the magnitude of the United States monetary commitment to Latin America *is* inadequate in view of the tremendous tasks which it must accomplish. This judgment, however, must be balanced against other considerations.

First of all, the United States impact upon Latin America does not lend itself to meaningful evaluation in terms of dollars and cents. The multiplicity of United States–Latin American human contacts and the flow of ideas that result therefrom are of enormous importance but defy accurate measurement. Even more fundamentally, it is difficult to argue that United States public-private efforts in Latin America must be intensified *unless* it can be demonstrated that the added commitment will produce the results desired. This is the crux of many a policy discussion in governmental councils as well as around the directorate boards of private companies and foundations when increased United States commitments to Latin America are being weighed.

In short, a greater United States effort in Latin America is needed but is difficult to stimulate, since the United States approach to Latin America has lacked three essential ingredients. It is these three ingredients upon which the United States policy maker must focus his attention:

1. A psychopolitical rationale that will unite United States and European public and private efforts and inspire greater Latin American participation in building a Triangular Atlantic Community of the West of which Latin America forms an integral part. An appropriate psychopolitical rationale has been suggested in Chapter 2, "The Atlantic Triangle."

2. A United States philosophy of action that combines realistic concepts of national power, operational tactics in the execution of policy, and an organizational framework within which an integrated public-private response toward Latin America can be formulated. This philosophy of action must suggest the leverage by which United States human and material resources might be committed to Latin America so as to produce the maximum effect. An appropriate United States philosophy of action has been suggested in Chapter 3, "The Operational Approach."

3. A clearly conceived set of priorities—an agenda for action which will concentrate United States energies on matters which merit most urgent attention.

Points 1 and 2 above have already been discussed at length. It is the third ingredient—point 3, the need for an agenda for action—which now merits attention.

9

Agenda

for

Action

A Strategy for the Americas must be considered at three levels. First, there is a grand design: the Atlantic Triangle idea which projects the vision of greater Western unity and Latin America's fuller identification with the modern West. Secondly, a Strategy for the Americas includes a philosophy of action to guide the United States in the pursuit of its objectives: an operational approach in which concepts of national power, tactical maneuverability, and organizational direction provide the motive power by which United States goals may be achieved. Thirdly, a Strategy for the Americas consists of specific proposals for policy action—immediate steps for attaining those objectives of highest priority. It is to this third level of strategy that we now turn.

A complete blueprint of the many options available to the United States policy maker will not be found in the proposals which follow. Instead, attention is focused on those leverage points of highest priority on which the United States should concentrate its energies.

The most important United States objectives in Latin America, it has been suggested, are defense of the Americas from hostile attack or internal subversion; development of an inter-American system capable of resolving United States–Latin American issues and coordinating political, economic, and other matters of mutual interest; and the application of the United

161

States public and private resources to Latin American modernization and integration within the modern West. It is within the context of these three major objectives that the proposals which follow are advanced.

I. Defense of the Americas

The bedrock of a United States Strategy for the Americas is the defense of the Organization of American States community from hostile attack—direct or indirect. Defense of the Americas requires not only conventional military preparedness but also positive measures to thwart Communist infiltration and subversion. Development goals clearly cannot be pursued at the necessary pace if Communist subversive activities divert the resources of Latin America from resolution of pressing economic problems and sow the seeds of discord among the Americas. The continued use of Cuba as a Communist base for subversion throughout the hemisphere and the concerted Communist effort to overthrow the Venezuelan government attest to the need for vigorous countermeasures. The following programs are essential:

A. *United States Military Assistance*

The United States Military Assistance Program (USMAP) in Latin America requires continued support. Although the need for conventional Latin American military forces equipped and trained to meet external attack has all but ceased, the need for units equipped and trained to maintain internal security and combat Communist insurgency has grown. Unfortunately, some irresponsible *golpes* (most of them carried out in the name of "internal security") have led to generalized but unjustified attacks on the USMAP as a whole. The Latin American military must project a more positive image. The USMAP's recent emphasis on civic-action programs in Latin America should contribute toward this end. The civic-action approach aims at orienting the Latin American military toward becoming an agent for constructive socioeconomic change. Thus, the USMAP's two principal aims are to increase counterinsurgency capabilities and enhance the civic-action potential of Latin America's armed forces. In view of the diversity in attitudes and capacities of individual Latin American military forces, the administration of the USMAP calls for the exercise of imagination, flexibility, and discretion. Tailor-made projects, stiff criteria for the distribution of military hardware, and careful vigilance over its use, and a readiness to reduce or shift the emphasis of United States assistance on the basis of demonstrated performance or changing needs are needed in this program.

The USMAP should channel support—given the necessary political decision of OAS membership—to help create an inter-American military force capable of responding to hemispheric crises, whether caused by Communist insurgency or violation of the principles covering human rights contained in the OAS Charter.

B. *Exchange of Information on Communist Activities*

Existing arrangements for the exchange of information on Communist activities and personalities in the Americas should be improved. If multilateral OAS action continues to prove deficient, supplementary limited multilateral or bilateral arrangements should be used more broadly to fill the void. As in all such matters, the effectiveness of this exchange program will probably be enhanced when the United States learns to employ more adroitly the art of political maneuver by rewarding its active supporters and showing less generosity to those whose cooperation in countering Communist subversion has been lacking.

C. *Effective Action against Castro's Cuba*

The continued existence of a Communist regime in Cuba is incompatible with United States and hemispheric security interests. Furthermore, Castro's dictatorship constitutes an impermissible infringement on the human rights of Cubans, including the right to express their popular will in free elections. Cuba's liberation must become a firm purpose of United States policy. United States coexistence with Communist Cuba must be clearly viewed as an interim relationship rather than a condition with which the United States will be content to live indefinitely. Cuba's liberation must be a goal to which the United States is dedicated unequivocally. Pending the attainment of that goal, an interim course must be charted.

Energetic and effective measures are needed to isolate the Castro regime. A diplomatic, economic, and informational offensive should be continued (with political action as an additional "persuader" if necessary) to convince nations of both North Atlantic Treaty Organization (NATO) and the OAS that the threat represented by a Communist Cuba is a threat to the West in general and to the inter-American system in particular. Cuba must be prevented from serving as a training, supply, and communications base for Communist efforts to disrupt Latin American development and to destroy inter-American harmony. Castro's aggression against the Venezuelan government and continued flaunting of the human rights of the Cuban people have put the OAS on trial as a mechanism for hemispheric defense and defender of self-determination. Should multilateral OAS action prove ineffective, the United States must then explore actively the possibilities of limited multilateral action by those nations of Latin America which share its estimate of the threat.

The precise nature of United States action vis-à-vis Communist Cuba must be tailored to an informed appraisal of the threat posed by Cuba at any given moment. Due account should be taken of the unfavorable impression created in Latin America by Castro's denial of human rights and the disastrous failures of Cuba's economic planning. Adequate account must also be taken of the fact that Castro's Cuba represents a drain on the Soviet economy which amounts to an estimated $1 million per day. A United States strategy of protracted conflict may best serve United States interests and eventually deal a blow to Soviet prestige in the Americas. The United States must neither overreact to the Cuban menace, nor must it ever again allow the development of such events as those which led to the missile crisis of October 1962.

Ultimately Cuba may present a threat to the hemisphere's security which will require the declaration of a naval blockade or even direct military action. Neither Havana nor Moscow should be given the impression that these options have been abandoned. Nor should the OAS be given the impression that the United States will allow its national security to be jeopardized while awaiting the development of a full multilateral consensus on how to deal with Castro. The United States must be prepared to take whatever action deemed necessary to meet the threat, based on a continuing and careful assessment of all relevant factors. An OAS consensus and joint action would be ideal, a limited multilateral action more feasible, but unilateral action —as President Kennedy made perfectly clear in his statement of April 20, 1961—provides an option which the United States cannot forego if the OAS system does not respond adequately to hemispheric defense needs.

D. *Reassessment of United States Military-Strategic Requirements*

There is an urgent need, as the United States approaches the 1970s, for reassessment of United States hemispheric military-strategic requirements in view of:

1. The missile-launching capabilities of Soviet submarines and the new weapons of the space age, particularly missiles of global range and orbital systems yet to become operational. These and other changing offensive-defensive considerations may alter current requirements for hemispheric defense.

2. Changing technology which may make necessary a fresh appraisal of United States requirements for strategic materials (particularly with respect to rare minerals) and the role of Latin America in supplying these needs.

3. Inadequate communication facilities linking the Americas, which point to the need for more secure and rapid communications which may be of vital importance during periods of crisis or hostilities. This need applies to United States diplomatic as well as military communications.

4. A sea-level canal to serve as an alternative route to the Panama Canal, which is deficient not only from the technical point of view but also vulnerable to political pressures.

Discussions already initiated with interested Latin American nations should include consideration of the desirability that new interocean canal projects be undertaken as joint inter-American ventures.

The reassessment of United States hemispheric military-strategic requirements on these four points may well influence a number of related United States policies such as the maintenance of strategic material stockpiles, the location and design of United States early warning systems, and the support of Latin American infrastructure projects such as road and railway links, port facilities, and communication networks.

II. Building an Effective Inter-American System

The organizational structure exists for achieving closer inter-American harmony and collaboration. Latin Americans wish to develop their human and material resources and can use foreign assistance to advantage. The United States possesses the will and many of the resources, human and material, needed to help Latin America speed its modernization. Yet important obstacles to effective inter-American collaboration persist. Fundamentally these obstacles are *human* in nature and will not respond to purely materialistic or mechanistic remedies. United States–Latin American issues are at their root psychological. Latin America's development is basically a matter of "changing the hearts and minds and capabilities of people."

Building a more effective inter-American system requires four essential steps:

1. United States analysis of Latin American problems with greater cultural empathy and with a willingness to diagnose the problems *before* writing prescriptions for their solution

2. Joint United States–Latin American efforts to overcome the psychological complexes which inevitably accompany the process of modernization so that Latin America may better absorb the human and material resources which the modern West can provide

3. A massive infusion into Latin America of the New Enlightenment of the modern West, with emphasis on the

need for changing basic human attitudes and improving human skills

4. An effort to link United States human and material resources to the enlightened leadership of Latin America's new elite through an operational approach employing the leverage of political action.

It is with these four requirements in mind that the following proposals are put forward.

A. *Increase United States Knowledge of Latin America*

There is an urgent need for a major public-private collaborative effort to increase United States knowledge of Latin America. United States private foundations, academic institutions, and a variety of other organizations, both public and private, should make a more *integrated response* to this need. Coordinated research programs with greater cross-fertilization of experience and centralization of information would make for a more systematic effort. Research should be focused upon problems of most vital concern to the Americas. Increased United States governmental support for this type of activity is both justified and required. The Latin American Strategy Board previously proposed could serve as a useful forum for increasing public-private collaboration in this field.

In the past, the United States has laid far more emphasis on prescriptions than diagnoses of the problems confronting Latin America. As a general commentary, the United States has often underestimated the *human* factor in the development equation. Support should be given to the study in greater depth of such questions as:

1. The process of cultural transition in Latin America, and methods by which the "culture shock" attending Latin America's entry into the modern West can be reduced

2. The cultural-value systems of Latin America and the effect of increased social mobility—e.g., the growing middle class—upon traditional values

3. Problems attending Latin America's rapid urbanization

4. Identification of leverage points important to the political actionist interested in promoting constructive socioeconomic change in Latin American society

5. Identification of new elite elements, such as those described in Chapter 4, which may provide the type of leadership which will both modernize and integrate more closely Latin American society

6. The requirements for generating an interdependent cycle of rural-urban growth

7. Ways and means of stimulating Latin American savings and channeling them into productive investments

These are but a few of the many subjects on which United States knowledge of Latin America is deficient. Others are suggested in proposals which follow.

B. *Psychological Persuasion: Building a Stronger Cultural Bridge*

Most United States–Latin American issues and many of the obstacles to Latin America's development are essentially psychological in nature. Both the United States private and public sectors must make a major effort to overcome these psychological barriers to better United States–Latin American understanding.

The USIA program in Latin America is generally well-oriented, but it requires a far greater United States investment in human and material resources. The magnitude of the problem of creating better understanding of the United States in Latin America has been gravely underestimated. More fundamentally, it is important to realize that—even if the USIA program should expand along its current lines—it would only scratch the surface. Basic and deeply rooted human attitudes must be changed as part of Latin America's modernization process. Deeply felt convictions must be created to identify Latin America with the dynamic values of the modern West. The United States government does not possess an organization with either the charter or resources for conducting the psychological engineering required to perform this difficult but essential task.[1] Whether such an effort should properly be combined with the activities now conducted by USIA is a matter of debate, but there is no question either that such a program is now lacking or that many reasons point to its need.

United States private business has dealt but superficially with the problem of influencing Latin American opinion on such questions as the function of capital, the profit motive, the nature of the modern mixed economy, and the necessity for raising productivity in order to support increased welfare programs. A sophisticated information effort must focus upon deeply rooted Iberian cultural attitudes. Marxian-inspired distortions, which stimulate much Latin American hostility toward United States business and the private enterprise system, must be analyzed to be combatted effectively. United States private enterprise must take greater responsibility and interest in informing Latin Americans about the true nature of the United States economic system. Programs to meet this need are likely to be far more effective if conducted through enlightened *Latin American* groups whose members share an interest in modernizing their countries by adopting from the dynamic economies of the modern West those features which most meet the needs of their countries.

C. *Transmitting the New Enlightenment of the Modern West*

Viewing the problems of Latin American development in their *human* perspective, the United States must make a more coordinated effort to spur the transmission of the New Enlightenment of the modern West to Latin America. Public-private collaborative efforts must disseminate more effectively the values and techniques of the modern West. United States foundations and academic institutions could make a considerable contribution toward this end. Efforts should be focused upon Latin America's fast-growing *urban centers* and on *youth.* The political-action potentialities of the intellectual-student tandem suggest that this group merits greater United States attention. Since members of Latin America's new elite are most likely to absorb and retrans-

[1] Cf. chap. 8 for an earlier discussion of psychological engineering.

mit the impulses of the modern West, they form a prime-target group.

Collaborative programs might combine private and public resources to help establish modern universities in key areas of Latin America. The University of the Andes provides a model for such institutions, since it combines a modern curriculum with a full-time and qualified faculty and nonpolitical direction. Greater support to institutions modeled after the United States land-grant colleges and to specialized vocational schools is also needed. A more energetic public-private collaborative effort should be made to increase the translation of selected English-language books and other materials into Spanish and Portuguese and to support their wider distribution in Latin America. The United States movie industry should be encouraged to raise the quality of the entertainment films and documentaries distributed in Latin America.

The need for a massive infusion of the values of the modern West into Latin America is clear. It is appropriate to reiterate that the Latin American Strategy Board recommended previously could serve as a useful forum for integrating the separate but complementary approaches needed to achieve this end.

D. *Linking United States Resources to Leadership of Latin America's New Elite*

As is true in so many other world areas, the power structure of Latin America is dominated by relatively few individuals. In some countries the dominant group is coincident with a traditional establishment which generally continues to resist the dynamic influences of the modern West and attempts to preserve the *status quo*. In most countries, however, an increasing number of persons with leadership potential are emerging to form a highly diverse group described previously as the new elite. It is with the enlightened elements of the new elite that the United States must create a collaborative tie. The linking of United States resources with the leadership abilities of Latin America's new elite suggests the formula most likely to effect Latin America's modernization and full participation in an Atlantic Community of the modern West. This formula, put more concretely, calls for an effective program of *political action* based on the realistic tenet that political maneuver is a fact of life and an essential element of statecraft. In programs of political action the United States should undertake activities wherever possible in conjunction with organized elements of Latin America's new elite. The above observations lead to two proposals:

1. Key United States officials responsible for the execution of United States policy should be trained in the art of political action—its potential, its varied operational channels, and its specific techniques. United States governmental institutions—e.g., the Foreign Service Institute, and the armed forces colleges and senior staff schools—should give great stress to this facet of statecraft, since it requires skills which have been largely foreign to United States tradition and experience. In addition, the United States Congress has before it three alternative bills calling for the establishment of a National Academy of Foreign Affairs, a United States Foreign Service Academy, and a Freedom Academy. Should favorable action be taken on any one of these three legislative proposals, provision should certainly be made for stressing the art of political action.

2. The prudent use of United States power strongly suggests that the United States attempt, whenever possible, to seek channels for *joint* United States–Latin American political action rather than attempt direct "wheeling and dealing" in the complex Latin American political milieu. There are Latin American leaders who share the United States objective of bolstering hemispheric defense against Communist subversion, who wish to establish an effective inter-American regional system, and who are striving to modernize their societies in ways which are compatible with United States interests and Western values. Such persons are members of Latin America's new elite. Thus, a prime requisite of effective United States political action calls for identifying new-elite elements in Latin America and encouraging them to carry out those measures needed to effect the modernization of their countries. Christian Democratic groups and elements

of Latin America's "democratic left" have already established institutes in which potential leaders receive training in political action. Hopefully, other segments of the non-Communist and democratically oriented political spectrum can be encouraged to do likewise. Latin American efforts of this type generally merit United States support and offer prospects of *joint*, or at least parallel, United States–Latin American political action.

III. Latin America's Development and Identification with the Modern West

An earlier review of United States public and private activities in Latin America supported the view that the United States exerts a powerful impact in speeding Latin America's modernization and closer identification with the modern West. This review also raised four points on which it is now appropriate to expand. First, some existing United States efforts to accelerate Latin America's economic growth might achieve greater success simply by placing heavier stress on the more positive aspects of existing programs, but particularly by effecting a more integrated public-private response. Secondly, granting the value to Latin America of current United States public-private activities, there is need for new and imaginative approaches in view of the enormous challenge of Latin America's development. Thirdly, greater self-help efforts must be generated from *within* Latin America, particularly by catalytic operations that unite human resources which are now dispersed. Fourthly, the magnitude of problems confronting Latin America's modernization demands an integrated response by those nations which constitute the Triangular Atlantic Community of the West. These four points form the framework for the proposals which follow:

A. *Increasing Effectiveness of Current United States Public and Private Activities*

1. The United States strategy for spurring Latin America's economic growth has the Alliance for Progress as its keystone. While the basic goals of the *Alianza* are sound, emphasis of the

following points would serve to increase the program's effectiveness:

a. The call in the Charter of Punta del Este for greater *productivity* should receive more stress. Productivity increases should precede the creation of expanded welfare programs. Social investments should concentrate upon those improvements which increase economic growth and productivity. An increase in Latin America's human capital is necessary. Greater expenditure for education to improve the knowledge and skills of Latin Americans is a prime task of the *Alianza.*

b. The national planning and government-to-government approaches of the *Alianza* must concentrate on harnessing Latin America's private capital resources as well as attracting a greater flow of foreign investment. The fact that the *Alianza* is dependent upon *private* Latin American and foreign capital sources for about 70 per cent of the funds for its ten-year program makes such an orientation mandatory.

c. There has been undue preoccupation with the *Alianza's* organizational structure. The existing structure will do whatever the collaborating governments want it to do. The decisions needed to invigorate the *Alianza* are basically *political.* A United States operational approach must employ effective political action in the *Alianza* program as well as in other activities. United States resources must be channeled to areas where they are most effectively employed and where a maximum degree of self-help effort is made.

d. When initially proposed, the *Alianza* was oversold with a promotional effort that gave undue emphasis to the role of the United States in providing capital and insufficient consideration to the need for general Latin American popular participation in a joint, long-range undertaking. Information programs must make greater efforts to correct this defect.

2. The image of youth portrayed by the United States Peace Corps—with its demonstration techniques, emphasis on community action, penetration into remote areas, and program flex-

ibility—has given rise to great hopes both in the United States and Latin America. It is important that this worthy program not be oversold, thus giving rise to expectations which cannot be fulfilled. The Peace Corps promises to make an important contribution to Latin America, but its effect can only be small when viewed in relation to the magnitude of Latin America's problems of modernization. The importance of the Peace Corps approach lies in its catalytic effect, i.e., the degree to which it stimulates Latin American self-help efforts of a similar nature.

3. United States business, an important transmitter of the ideas of the modern West, must expand current efforts to cultivate in its field representatives greater cultural empathy toward Latin America. It must demonstrate increased willingness to merge its enterprises into Latin American economies by giving greater emphasis to joint United States–Latin American ventures. As mentioned previously, the need also exists for a more profound and sophisticated public relations campaign that will dispose Latin Americans more favorably toward United States business.

4. Activities undertaken by the United States public and private sectors in Latin America reveal the unfortunate lack of an integrated approach. The diffusion of effort has weakened what would otherwise be a much greater United States impact. United States public and private resources must be more effectively combined to exert greater leverage in speeding Latin American development. Once again, the need for a forum such as that proposed earlier, the Latin American Strategy Board, is apparent.

B. *The Injection of United States Capital, Organizational Skills, and Technology*

In addition to the broad range of activities already pursued by the United States public and private sectors in Latin America, there are additional approaches which the United States might adopt to speed Latin America's modernization. Three such approaches are as follows:

1. *Inter-American Development Corporation.* An Inter-American Development Corporation (IADC) could be established as a private United States corporate entity through which capital (private and public, United States and foreign) might be in-

vested to stimulate the development of key sectors in the Latin American economy.[2] As a matter of basic policy IADC activities should be oriented toward sparking new approaches and joint United States–Latin American ventures rather than settling into competitive efforts in conventional commercial fields. Such an approach would require topflight managerial talent and should be designed to attract the individual investor by public stock offerings. The IADC might conduct direct operations in new fields (similar to the approach of the International Basic Economy Corporation), or might invest in individual and corporate ventures (similar to the Creole Investment Corporation). Community development corporations, cooperative groups, development banks or *financieras* would be eligible applicants for IADC direct investment or credit. The proposed IADC would merit consideration for special tax concessions and investment guarantees backed by the United States government, since it would provide capital for risk ventures and catalytic operations. One of the most important functions of the IADC might be that of a private contractor and chosen instrument for administering publicly financed aid programs which in many instances may be carried out more efficiently when removed from the bureaucratic channels of government-to-government operations. In this function, the IADC could serve in the field of foreign aid as the private arm of a new and imaginative United States operational approach. A development corporation such as the IADC might attract a substantial amount of Latin American capital which now flows to markets outside this hemisphere.

2. *Harnessing the potential of senior United States consultant talent.* There is a growing reservoir of senior or retired United States citizens who possess outstanding managerial, technical, and

[2] Cf. chap. 2. ADELA embodies some of the features of the proposed IADC but does not possess the scale (capital of $32 million by mid-1965), United States corporate status (with its attendant benefits), or appeal to the individual investor envisioned for the IADC. On the other hand, ADELA's multinational character may better enable it to tap extrahemispheric capital sources and fulfill a function for which the IADC is not as well suited. Consequently, the IADC and ADELA can be regarded as complementary rather than competitive efforts.

other talents which can be brought to bear on key problems of
Latin America's development. This group is composed of former
diplomats, other former United States public servants, retired
United States businessmen, engineers, senior academicians, sci-
entists, financiers, marketing experts and so on.[3] Some among this
diverse group are rich in Latin American area experience while
others have functional specialities needed to spur the region's
economic growth. Many are "idea men" in addition to their technical competence. While their potential has already been tapped
in part—especially by United States governmental and international agencies—the full contribution they are capable of making
(for the most part on a *gratis* or expense-paid basis) has simply
not been solicited in any systematic fashion. The Latin American
Strategy Board is the logical point for an examination of the means
by which senior United States consultant talent might be utilized.
The imaginative and catalytic public-private approaches which
such talent might be expected to develop would, of course, be
more likely to result from an atmosphere which encouraged complete objectivity and maximum freedom of action. The type of
investigations which a senior consultants corps such as proposed
above might undertake would include the following:

a. Novel and imaginative approaches to the use of United
States capital and technical skills in the modernization of
Latin America are much in need. For example, the advance
of automation in the United States is causing the retirement
of billions of dollars worth of industrial equipment which
might be adaptable to the needs of Latin America. In many
cases, the United States technician who is skilled in operating and maintaining this equipment is also "retired" to the
ranks of the unemployed in the United States, or becomes
the subject of costly "retraining" programs. There are good
prospects for joint United States–Latin American ventures
which combine the used capital equipment and the technical skill of a United States firm with the local capital and

[3] The International Executive Service Corps (IESC) discussed previously
is similar in general concept but considerably more narrow in membership
and function. The IESC and the above proposal are essentially parallel but
noncompetitive approaches.

marketing knowledge of Latin American entrepreneurs. Thus, human and material resources might be transferred "as a package" under conditions which are commercially sound and yield a considerable foreign exchange saving to Latin America. This approach would seem particularly adaptable to medium-sized United States and Latin American firms.

b. More resource inventories, market analyses, and promotional activities to develop and expand markets for relatively unknown or inadequately exploited Latin American products are needed. For example, there are a variety of tropical fruits which, in fresh or processed forms, might have considerable market appeal in the United States or Europe if promoted. Latin American fibers and precious woods have been only partially exploited. Latin Americans, however, frequently lack knowledge of world market possibilites and the techniques for exploiting them. On the other hand, entrepreneurs and prospective investors in the United States sometimes do not perceive the resource potential. Again, there is a need for a bridge to link the potential and its effective exploitation.

c. Possibilities for generating within Latin America a more dynamic process of private capital accumulation and investment must be explored more actively, e.g., promoting additional private development banks or *financieras;* promoting savings and loan associations in areas where they have not yet been introduced; and assisting in setting up local stock markets where the volume of private corporate business suggests the need for such a financial institution.

d. The problem of generating an interdependent cycle of rural-urban growth in Latin America is a crucial one which merits the attention of highly qualified United States consultants to explore varied approaches, e.g., better marketing of Latin American agricultural products in the urban centers; production and distribution within Latin American rural areas of simple and low-cost agricultural equipment and consumer goods; and the expansion of agricultural cooperatives. The problem, of course, varies from region to region. In brief, there is an urgent need for developing national economies within Latin America.

3. *Harnessing the potential of modern technology.* Enormous United States scientific research facilities, public and private, are engaged in many investigations which have relevance to Latin America's problems of development. The allocation of greater resources or the granting of higher priority to certain selected research programs might lead to breakthroughs which would hasten the modernization of Latin America as well as other less developed regions. Many scientific research programs tailored to United States requirements have neither the sense of immediacy nor the impetus required to meet Latin America's needs. The following projects are illustrative of those which merit high priority:

a. The use of atomic energy for controlled power, with special reference to transportable atomic generators; the development of atomic-blasting techniques for creating ports, reducing highway and railway engineering costs, digging canals (e.g., an alternate to the Panama Canal), and building hydroelectric and irrigation facilities

b. The conversion of sea water to fresh water, a development which might well be linked to research on lower-cost atomic energy, while at the same time contributing greatly to Latin America's agrarian productivity

c. The elimination of hoof and mouth disease (aftosa) which has affected adversely the prospects of Latin American beef exports

d. Improvements in the communications systems linking the Americas

e. The control and elimination of tropical diseases

f. The development of inexpensive and acceptable methods of birth control

g. The development of such vehicles as hovercraft, hydrofoils, and ground-effect machines for use in areas where the initial capital expenditure required to construct roadbeds and bridges would be prohibitively high

h. Special design of equipment and manufacturing processes with emphasis on simplicity of operation, durability, minimal maintenance requirements, and small-volume markets

i. Improved methods for the exploitation, preservation, and processing of fruit and fish products

j. Development of low-cost construction materials and techniques, with particular reference to Latin America's housing problems

C. *Latin American Self-Help: National Development Corps*

It is difficult to overemphasize the need for self-help programs of development in Latin America. Approximately 90 per cent of the gross investment made in Latin America comes from public and private sources within the area. In addition, self-help programs build self-respect, thus providing a healthier atmosphere within which Latin Americans can absorb the impulses of the modern West without developing those negative psychological reactions which have impeded their progress in the past.

Taking account of these and other considerations, the United States public and private sectors should join in stimulating and assisting in the formation of a series of National Development Corps (Cuerpos Nacionales de Desarrollo). Such organizations could combine the civic-action programs undertaken by Latin American military forces and the activities of local Latin American Peace Corps units. National Development Corps could harness the energies of the migrants now moving from rural areas of Latin America to overcrowded urban centers which are not prepared to give them either employment or adequate public services. As the Latin American agrarian sector modernizes and becomes more productive, the exodus of rural workers to urban centers is likely to grow. Unless the energies of these migrants are absorbed in the type of projects which a National Development Corps might undertake, serious unemployment and social discontent could result. A considerable number of skilled persons including engineers, physicians, medical technicians, and economists are emigrating from Latin America. This exodus of skilled citizens represents in some countries a loss of human resources which Latin America can ill afford. Attempts should be made to convert this "brain drain" into leadership cadres within the National Development Corps. It would require the imagination and full dedication of many members of Latin America's new elite. The possibilities for success in this approach, however, make the undertaking worthwhile. National Development Corps might logically concentrate on such projects as building rail lines, road networks, hydroelectric facilities, rural schools and clinics, urban renewal, resource inventories, and low-cost housing. Some of these projects would focus on the construction of the broader Latin American infrastructure base upon which private investors might build. Aside from the prospective tangible accomplishments of the National Development Corps, the very effort itself would provide Latin America with invaluable experience in the type of collaborative effort which fosters greater national cohesion.

National Development Corps warrant the support of the *Alianza*. Specific projects undertaken by such Corps might qualify for IADB financing or obtain financial assistance from other international institutions. The diversity of Latin America is such that the structure and purpose of National Development Corps would probably vary considerably in accordance with local needs. But the general approach would represent a dramatic demonstration of the self-help efforts without which proposals for foreign assistance made elsewhere in this chapter would have a hollow ring.

D. *Atlantic Triangle Action*

1. As a matter of highest national policy, the United States should make a major effort to concentrate the resources of the modern West on speeding Latin America's development and fuller integration into a Triangular Atlantic Community. The formation of European and Latin American organizations, public and private, which share this objective merit encouragement and support. The Development Advisory Committee (DAC) of the Organization for Economic Cooperation and Development

might serve as a focal point for coordinating aid from North Atlantic countries to Latin America.

2. The United States should attempt to shift assistance to Latin America from capital transfusions and "bailout" loans to the healthier economic base of increased commercial interchange. Greater dedication to the principles of comparative economic advantage both at home and abroad and less inclination to yield to the pressure of vested interests is needed, as well as the creation of conditions more favorable to the investment of North American and European private capital in Latin America. The problem is triangular and cannot be approached realistically unless there is a willingness to make concessions as well as realize advantages. The practical political difficulties in effecting reciprocal concessions—such as those contained in the recommendations which follow—are recognized. But they must be met head on by enlightened and courageous leadership. A broad Atlantic Triangle approach to reduce the obstacles to freer trade and investment should be vigorously pursued. This would necessitate concessions along these general lines:

a. The United States should grant increased access to its domestic markets for low-cost, efficient, free-world producers of copper, lead, zinc, petroleum, sugar, wool, beef, and possibly a selected group of semimanufactured products. The operation of the Public Law 480 program should be continually assessed to assure that United States subsidization of its domestic agricultural sector does not damage other free world economies. United States concessions of this nature could result in increased Latin American exports amounting from $1.5 to $2 billion annually, not to mention the incalculable psychological boost represented by Latin America's increased sense of *earning* its way by trade rather than depending upon continued United States aid. Increased European trade with and investment in Latin America should be encouraged. Latin American recipients of United States aid funds should have greater authority to buy from European suppliers, especially when the latter are clearly lower cost producers than United States competitors. In short, preachments of "free market" and "comparative advantage" are not effective unless practiced. The United States concessions recommended are predicated, of course, on equalizing concessions from the other two corners of the Triangle (such as those outlined below). If equivalent concessions were not forthcoming, various arguments (e.g., unfavorable balance in payments) would no doubt be advanced to justify continued United States protectionism.

b. The European Economic Community and other European nations should be encouraged to grant freer access to their markets for Latin American exports. The reduction of internal consumption taxes in some European countries would have a salutary effect upon the sales of some Latin American exports. United States concessions opening Latin American markets to European exporters by permitting greater use of United States aid funds for European purchases must be matched by European concessions liberalizing the entry of United States products to their trading areas.

c. Latin Americans must be encouraged to avoid excessive protectionist measures in their common market arrangements, to make more effective use of foreign aid and credits, and to reexamine those portions of their import substitution program which are inconsistent (even in the long run) with the rationale of comparative advantage. Furthermore, Latin America should make energetic efforts to attract foreign private investments by providing adequate inducements and assuring fair treatment. The UN Conference on Trade and Development held in Geneva from March to June 1964 should have made it clear to Latin America that concrete self-help measures must be combined with realistic give-and-take negotiations with the North Atlantic trading area if Latin America's export income is to be expanded. The Conference also should have provided evidence of the futility of efforts to form a Latin American–Asian–African "have-not" bloc capable of obtaining "guaranteed market access," "special and nonreciprocal concessions," and other advantages for which the have-nots have insufficient bargaining power vis-à-vis the more advanced countries of the West.

3. The North Atlantic powers, preferably by joint action in the Development Advisory Council of the OECD, should give special attention to the fluctuations which affect the sales of, and income from, certain primary products. This is *not* to suggest general adoption of commodity-stabilization schemes urged by many primary-product producers. There is little in the history of commodity-stabilization agreements to suggest that they can provide an acceptable long-range solution to the basic problems of primary-producing countries. However, compensation agreements—closely tied to, and made conditional upon, certain concrete actions to be taken by the primary producers benefited—merit consideration in the United States and Western Europe. Such agreements can provide for what are essentially countercyclical loans which have as their objective basic structural changes within the economy of primary-producing nations. Compensation agreements are designed to reduce, if not eliminate in time, the reliance of primary-commodity producers upon continued assistance of this type; they help to build a freer market which will give greater play to the law of comparative advantage. There are numerous technical difficulties to this approach, but it deserves careful study and consideration.

4. Inelastic demand for or supply of primary commodities in the world market presents one of the principal economic problems of Latin America. While it is unlikely that these inherent features of commodity trade can be eliminated, the creation of a centralized market-reporting mechanism might help to reduce their harmful effects upon primary-producing nations. The DAC might perform such a function. Improved long-range meteorological forecasts, modern worldwide communications, and automated data processing should be combined to reduce the inelasticity which has characterized primary-commodity markets.

5. North Atlantic and Latin American countries should give urgent attention to the creation of an Atlantic Triangle investors' convention. A multilateral understanding would encourage Europeans and North American private interests to consider invest-

ing in Latin America with assurance that they were not entering a game the rules of which could be changed without notice. Latin Americans would have an opportunity to clarify the measures they deem necessary to protect their national interests. The framers of such a convention should make a concerted effort to provide acceptable standards for expropriation settlement, capital remittances, and other matters affecting investment in Latin America. The DAC or the OECD might again serve as an appropriate forum for the drafting of an Atlantic Triangle investor's convention. Conceivably, OECD equity courts might adjudicate disputes which arise under this convention.

Conclusion

The foregoing proposals suggest priorities that merit concentrated efforts on the part of the United States as well as other nations of the modern West. Many of these proposals face difficult obstacles. Some will meet the strong opposition of vested interests. Others would require decades to produce significant results. While the actions proposed can be expected to work no miracles, their adoption would represent important steps in a long and difficult process of building greater Western unity.

The impact of modernization upon Latin America has provided a dramatic story of Western dynamism. As in other world areas, the process of Westernization has been an arduous one, often accompanied by revolutionary changes and adverse psychological reactions. Latin Americans will welcome some but, understandably, resist other influences from the modern West. In varying degrees, they are of the West, but with a difference. They admire the accomplishments of the modern West but often resist the adoption of those attitudes, institutions, and techniques by which the West achieved its way of life. They would, if they could, have the best of two worlds. Conflicting values, however, deny Latin Americans this possibility. It is this clash that is so characteristic of the worldwide impact of Western dynamism on other societies. In the end, the decision will be theirs.

The West can no more withdraw and cease to transmit the New Enlightenment than can Latin America resist the quickening impulses of modernization. Thus, the question really becomes one of not *if* but *how* the United States and other nations of the modern West should exert their influences on a Latin America in the throes of cultural transition. The answer for the West lies in recognizing the power and attraction of its way of life, but displaying cultural empathy, patience, and tolerance for diversity.

Latin America's identification with the West and its closer integration within a Triangular Atlantic Community defines the central goal of a Strategy for the Americas. This vision of greater Western unity confronts many countercurrents. But it is the function of strategy to mold rather than to conform to human events. The future will be won by those who, within the limits of human action, are willing to look beyond the horizon of their times to chart their course.

Selected

Bibliography

Adams, Mildred (ed.): *Latin America: Evolution or Explosion?* Dodd, Mead & Company, Inc., New York, 1963.

Adams, Richard N., et al.: *Social Change in Latin America Today: Its Implications for United States Policy*, Vintage Books, Random House, Inc., for the Council on Foreign Relations, New York, 1960.

―――― and Charles C. Cumberland: *United States University Cooperation in Latin America*, Institute of Research on Overseas Programs, Michigan State University, East Lansing, Mich., 1960.

Aitken, Thomas: *A Foreign Policy for American Business*, Harper & Brothers, New York, 1962.

Alba, Victor: *La América latina y los congresos del partido comunista ruso*, Imprenta Vargas, San José, Costa Rica, n.d.

――――: *Historia del comunismo en América latina*, Ediciones Occidentales, Mexico, 1960.

――――: *El Militarismo*, Instituto de Investigaciones Sociales, Universidad Nacional Autónoma de México, Mexico, 1959.

Alexander, Robert J.: *The Bolivian National Revolution*, Rutgers University Press, New Brunswick, N.J., 1958.

――――:*Communism in Latin America*, Rutgers University Press, New Brunswick, N.J., 1957.

――――:*Prophets of the Revolution*, The Macmillan Company, New York, 1962.

Allen, Robert Loring: *Soviet Influence in Latin America: The Role of Economic Relations*, Public Affairs Press, Washington, D.C., 1959.

Almond, Gabriel A., and James S. Coleman (eds.): *The Politics of the Developing Areas*, Princeton University Press, Princeton, N.J., 1960.

The American Assembly: *The United States and Latin America*, Columbia University, New York, 1959.

Anderson, Charles W., and William P. Glade, Jr.: *The Political Economy of Mexico*, The University of Wisconsin Press, Madison, Wis., 1963.

Arévalo, Juan José: *AntiKomunismo en América latina*, Editorial Palestra, Buenos Aires, 1959.

187

————: *The Shark and the Sardines,* Lyle Stuart, New York, 1961.

Arnade, Charles W.: *The Emergence of the Republic of Bolivia,* University of Florida Press, Gainesville, Fla., 1957.

Artime Buesa, Manuel: *Traición!* Editorial Jus, Mexico, 1960.

Asher, Robert E.: *Development of the Emerging Countries,* The Brookings Institution, Washington, D.C., 1962.

————: *Grants, Loans, and Local Currencies,* The Brookings Institution, Washington, D.C., 1961.

Bailey, Helen M., and Abraham P. Nasatir: *Latin America: The Development of its Civilization,* Prentice-Hall, Inc., Englewood Cliffs, N.J., 1960.

Bauer, Raymond, et al.: *American Business and Public Policy,* Atherton Press, New York, 1963.

Bemis, Samuel Flagg: *The Latin American Policy of the United States,* Harcourt, Brace & World, Inc., New York, 1943.

Benham, F.: *A Short Introduction to the Economy of Latin America,* Royal Institute of International Affairs, London, 1960.

Benton, William F.: *The Voice of Latin America,* Harper & Row, Publishers, Incorporated, New York, 1961.

Berle, Adolph A.: *Latin America: Diplomacy and Reality,* Harper & Row, Publishers, Incorporated, New York, 1962.

Brandenburg, Frank: *The Development of Latin American Private Enterprise,* National Planning Association, Washington, D.C., 1964.

Burgess, Eugene W., and Frederick H. Harbison: *Casa Grace in Peru,* National Planning Association, Washington, D.C., 1954.

Burnett, Ben G., and Moisés Poblete Troncoso: *The Rise of the Latin American Labor Movement,* Bookman Associates, New York, 1960.

The Capital Development Needs of the Less Developed Countries, United Nations, Department of Public Information, New York, 1962.

Cline, Howard F.: *Mexico: Revolution to Evolution, 1940–1960,* Oxford University Press, London, 1962.

Coffey, Joseph I., and Vincent P. Rock: *The Presidential Staff,* National Planning Association Washington D.C., 1961.

Cosío Villegas, Daniel: *Change in Latin America: The Mexican and Cuban Revolutions,* University of Nebraska Press, Lincoln, Nebr., 1961.

Crawford, W. Rex: *A Century of Latin-American Thought,* Harvard University Press, Cambridge, Mass., 1961.

Cuevas Cancino, Francisco: *Del Congreso de Panamá a la Conferencia de Caracas, 1826–1954*, vol. II, Caracas, 1955.

D'Antonio, William V., and Frederick B. Pike (eds.): *Religion, Revolution, and Reform: New Forces for Change in Latin America*, Frederick A. Praeger, Inc., New York, 1964.

Davis, Harold E.: *Government and Politics in Latin America*, The Ronald Press Company, New York, 1958.

Delwart, Louis O.: *The Future of Latin American Exports to the United States: 1965 and 1970*, National Planning Association, Washington, D.C., 1960.

Deriabin, Peter, and Frank Gibney: *The Secret World*, Doubleday & Company, Inc., Garden City, N.Y., 1959.

Díaz Cisneros, César: *Derecho internacional público*, vol. I, Tipográfica Editora, Buenos Aires, 1955.

Dizard, Wilson P.: *The Strategy of Truth: The Story of the U.S. Information Agency*, Public Affairs Press, Washington, D.C., 1961.

Dodd, Thomas J.: *Freedom and Foreign Policy*, The Bookmailer, Inc., New York, 1962.

Donovan, John: *Red Machete: Communist Infiltration in the Americas*, The Bobbs-Merrill Company, Inc., Indianapolis, 1962.

Dozer, Donald M.: *Latin America: An Interpretative History*, McGraw-Hill Book Company, New York, 1962.

Draper, Theodore: *Castroism: Theory and Practise*, Frederick A. Praeger, Inc., New York, 1963.

Dreier, John C. (ed.): *The Alliance for Progress*, The Johns Hopkins Press, Baltimore, 1962.

———: *The Organization of American States and the Hemispheric Crisis*, Harper & Row, Publishers, Incorporated, for the Council on Foreign Relations, New York, 1962.

The Economic Development of Latin America in the Post-War Period, vol. II, United Nations, Mar del Plata, Argentina, 1963.

Economic Survey of Latin America 1958, United Nations, Geneva, 1957.

The Effects of the European Economic Community on the Latin American Economies, Pan American Union, Washington, D.C., 1963.

Eisenhower, Milton S.: *The Wine is Bitter*, Doubleday & Company, Inc., Garden City, N.Y., 1963.

Elder, Robert E.: *The Policy Machine*, Syracuse University Press, Syracuse, N.Y., 1960.

Ellis, H. C. (ed.): *Economic Development for Latin America*, St. Martin's Press, Inc., New York, 1961.

✓ Ellis, Howard S., et al.: *The Teaching of Economics in Latin America*,

Report to UNESCO, ECLA, and the OAS, Pan American Union, Washington, D.C., 1963.

Energy in Latin America, United Nations, Geneva, 1957.

La Estructura demográfica de las naciones americanas, vol. I, II, Pan American Union, Washington, D.C., 1960, 1959.

Europe's Role in Latin American Development, Inter-American Development Bank, Buenos Aires, 1962.

First Annual Meeting of the Inter-American Economic and Social Council at the Ministerial Level, Pan American Union, Washington, D.C., 1963.

Flores, Edmundo: *Land Reform and the Alliance for Progress,* Policy Memorandum No. 27, Center of International Studies, Princeton University, Princeton, N.J., 1963.

Ford, Thomas R.: *Man and Land in Peru,* University of Florida Press, Gainesville, Fla., 1962.

Foreign Capital In Latin America, United Nations, Department of Public Information, New York, 1955.

Foreign Private Investments in the Latin American Free-Trade Area, United Nations, Department of Public Information, New York, 1961.

Franco, Victor: *The Morning After,* Frederick A. Praeger, Inc., New York, 1963.

Freyre, Gilberto: *Masters and Slaves,* Alfred A. Knopf, Inc., New York, 1946.

————: *New World in the Tropics,* Alfred A. Knopf, Inc., New York, 1959.

Fritsch, William R.: *Progress and Profits,* Action Committee for International Development, Washington, D.C., 1962.

Furtado, Celso: *The Economic Growth of Brazil,* R. W. de Aguiar and E. C. Drysdale (trans.), University of California Press, Berkeley, Calif., 1963.

Geiger, Theodore: *The General Electric Company in Brazil,* National Planning Association, Washington, D.C., 1961.

Geisert, Harold L.: *World Population Pressures,* The George Washington University Press, 1958.

Germani, Gino: *Estructura social de la Argentina,* Editorial Raigel, Buenos Aires, 1955.

Glick, Philip M.: *The Administration of Technical Assistance: Growth in the Americas,* The University of Chicago Press, Chicago, 1957.

Gómez Robledo, Antonio: *Idea y experiencia de América,* Fondo de Cultura Económica, Mexico, 1958.

Gordon, Lincoln: *A New Deal for Latin America*, Harvard University Press, Cambridge, Mass., 1963.

———— and Engelbert L. Grommers: *United States Manufacturing Investment in Brazil*, Center for International Affairs, Harvard University, Cambridge, Mass., 1962.

Graber, D. A.: *Crisis Diplomacy*, Public Affairs Press, Washington, D.C., 1959.

Guevara, Ernesto "Che": *Guerrilla Warfare*, Monthly Review Press, New York, 1961.

Hanke, Lewis (ed.): *Have the Americas a Common History?* Alfred A. Knopf, Inc., New York, 1964.

————: *Mexico and the Caribbean*, D. Van Nostrand Company, Inc., Princeton, N.J., 1959.

————: *South America*, D. Van Nostrand Company, Inc., Princeton, N.J., 1959.

Hauser, Philip M. (ed.): *Urbanization in Latin America*, International Documents Service, Columbia University Press, New York, 1961.

Haviland, H. Field, Jr.: *The Formulation and Administration of United States Foreign Policy*, The Brookings Institution, Washington, D.C., 1960.

Hearings before the Senate Committee on Foreign Relations, The Operational Aspects of U.S. Foreign Policy, 86th Cong., 1st Sess., 1959.

Hearings before the Senate Committee on Foreign Relations, Summary of Views of Retired Foreign Service Officers, 86th Cong., 1st Sess., 1959.

Hearings before the Senate Committee on Foreign Relations, Training of Foreign Affairs Personnel, 88th Cong., 1st Sess., 1963.

Hearings before the Subcommittee on National Policy Machinery of the Committee on Government Operations, National Policy Machinery in the Soviet Union, 86th Cong., 2d. Sess., 1960.

Hearings before the Subcommittee on National Policy Machinery of the Committee on Government Operations, Organizing for National Security, 87th Cong., 1st Sess., 1961.

Herring, Hubert: *A History of Latin America*, Harper & Brothers, New York, 1961.

Hirschman, Albert O.: *Journeys Toward Progress*, The Twentieth Century Fund, New York, 1963.

———— (ed.): *Latin American Issues*, The Twentieth Century Fund, New York, 1961.

————: *The Strategy of Economic Development*, Yale University Press, New Haven, Conn., 1960.

Huberman, Leo, and Paul M. Sweezy: *Cuba: Anatomy of a Revolution*, Monthly Review Press, New York, 1961.

Hunter, John M.: *Emerging Colombia*, Public Affairs Press, Washington, D.C., 1962.

The International Bank for Reconstruction and Development: *The Economic Development of Venezuela*, The Johns Hopkins Press, Baltimore, 1961.

The International Flow of Private Capital, 1956–1958, United Nations, Department of Public Information, New York, 1959.

James, Daniel: *Red Design for the Americas*, The John Day Company, Inc., New York, 1954.

Johnson, John J. (ed.): *The Role of the Military in Underdeveloped Countries*, Princeton University Press, Princeton, N.J., 1962.

————: *Political Change in Latin America*, Stanford University Press, Stanford, Calif., 1958.

Kautsky, John H. (ed.): *Political Change in Underdeveloped Countries: Nationalism and Communism*, John Wiley & Sons, Inc., New York, 1962.

Kintner, William R., and Joseph Z. Kornfeder: *The New Frontier of War*, Henry Regnery Company, Chicago, 1962.

Kubitschek, Juscelino: *Report on the Alliance for Progress*, Pan American Union, Washington, D.C., 1963.

Lauerhass, Ludwig, Jr. (ed.): *Communism in Latin America: A Bibliography*, Center for Latin American Studies, University of California, Los Angeles, 1962.

Lieuwen, Edwin: *Arms and Politics in Latin America*, Frederick A. Praeger, Inc., New York, 1961.

————: *Generals vs. Presidents: Neomilitarism in Latin America*, Frederick A. Praeger, Inc., New York, 1964.

Lleras Camargo, Alberto: *Report on the Alliance for Progress*, Pan American Union, Washington, D.C., 1963.

Madariaga, Salvador de: *Latin America between the Eagle and the Bear*, Frederick A. Praeger, Inc., New York, 1962.

Maddox, James G.: *Technical Assistance by Religious Agencies in Latin America*, The University of Chicago Press, Chicago, 1956.

Mair, Joseph, and Richard W. Weatherhead (eds.): *Politics of Change in Latin America*, Frederick A. Praeger, Inc., New York, 1965.

Manger, William: *Pan America in Crisis*, Public Affairs Press, Washington, D.C., 1961.

Martz, John D.: *Central America*, The University of North Carolina Press, Chapel Hill, N.C., 1959.

——: *Colombia*, The University of North Carolina Press, Chapel Hill, N.C., 1962.

May, Stacy, and Galo Plaza: *The United Fruit Company in Latin America*, National Planning Association, Washington, D.C., 1958.

Mecham, J. Lloyd: *The United States and Inter-American Security, 1889–1960*, University of Texas Press, Austin, Tex., 1962.

Meyer, Karl E., and Tad Szulc: *The Cuban Invasion*, Frederick A. Praeger, Inc., New York, 1962.

Millen, Bruce H.: *The Political Role of Labor in Developing Countries*, The Brookings Institution, Washington, D.C., 1963.

Monahan, James, and Kenneth O. Gilmore: *The Great Deception*, Farrar, Straus & Co., New York, 1963.

Mosher, Arthur T.: *Technical Co-operation in Latin-American Agriculture*, The University of Chicago Press, Chicago, 1957.

Neale, Alan D.: *The Flow of Resources from Rich to Poor*, Center for International Affairs, Harvard University, Cambridge, Mass., 1961.

Nehemkis, Peter: *Latin America: Myth and Reality*, Alfred A. Knopf, Inc., New York, 1964.

Nurske, Ragnar: *Problems of Capital Formation in Underdeveloped Countries*, Oxford University Press, Fair Lawn, N.J., 1962.

The Old World and the New World: Their Cultural and Moral Relations, UNESCO, United Nations, Paris, 1956.

Ornes, Germán C.: *Trujillo: Little Caesar of the Caribbean*, Thomas Nelson & Sons, New York, 1958.

Palacios, Alfredo L.: *Nuestra América y el imperialismo*, Editorial Palestra, Buenos Aires, 1961.

Palmer, Thomas W., Jr.: *Search for a Latin American Policy*, University of Florida Press, Gainesville, Fla., 1957.

Pellecer, Carlos Manuel: *Renuncia al comunismo*, Costa-Amic, Mexico, 1963.

Pérez Guerrero, Alfredo: *Ecuador*, Casa de la Cultura Ecuatoriana, Quito, Ecuador, 1948.

Perkins, Dexter: *Hands Off: A History of the Monroe Doctrine*, Little, Brown and Company, Boston, 1941.

Picón-Salas, Mariano: *A Cultural History of Spanish America*, Irving A. Leonard (trans.), University of California Press, Berkeley, 1962.

Pike, Frederick B.: *Chile and the United States, 1880–1962*, University of Notre Dame Press, Notre Dame, Ind., 1963.

Plaza, Galo: *Problems of Democracy in Latin America*, The University of North Carolina Press, Chapel Hill, N.C., 1955.

Poppino, Rollie E.: *International Communism in Latin America: A History of the Movement, 1917–1963*, The Free Press of Glencoe, New York, 1964.

Porter, Charles O., and Robert J. Alexander: *The Struggle for Democracy in Latin America*, The Macmillan Company, New York, 1961.

Powelson, John P.: *Latin America: Today's Economic and Social Revolution*, McGraw-Hill Book Company, New York, 1964.

Priest, A. R.: *Public Finance in Underdeveloped Countries*, Frederick A. Praeger, Inc., New York, 1962.

Quintanilla, Luis: *A Latin American Speaks*, The Macmillan Company, New York, 1943.

✓ Radler, D. H.: *El Gringo: The Yankee Image in Latin America*, Chilton Company—Book Division, Philadelphia, 1962.

Randall, Clarence B.: *The Communist Challenge to American Business*, Little, Brown and Company, Boston, 1959.

Raushenbush, Stephen: *The Challenge to the Alliance for Progress*, Public Affairs Press, Washington, D.C., 1962.

Ravines, Eudocio: *The Yenan Way*, Charles Scribner's Sons, New York, 1951.

Report on the Situation Regarding Human Rights in the Dominican Republic, Pan American Union, Washington, D.C., 1962.

Report on the Situation Regarding Human Rights in Haiti, Pan American Union, Washington, D.C., 1963.

Report on the Situation Regarding Human Rights in the Republic of Cuba, Pan American Union, Washington, D.C., 1962.

Report on the World Social Situation 1963, United Nations, Department of Public Information, New York, 1964.

Rodó, José Enrique: *Ariel*, Houghton Mifflin Company, Boston, 1922.

Rodríguez-Aria Bustamante, Lino: *La Democracia cristiana y América latina*, Editorial Universitaria, Lima, Peru, 1961.

Romero, José Luis: *Las Ideas políticas en Argentina*, Fondo de Cultura Económica, Mexico, 1946.

Rostow, W. W.: *The Stages of Economic Growth*, Cambridge University Press, London, 1961.

Rottenberg, Simon: *How United States Business Firms Promote Tech-*

nological Progress, National Planning Association, Washington, D.C., 1957.

Schmitt, Karl M., and David D. Burks: *Evolution or Chaos? Dynamics of Latin American Government and Politics,* Frederick A. Praeger, Inc., New York, 1963.

✓Schultz, Theodore, W.: *The Economic Test in Latin America,* Bulletin No. 35, New York State School of Industrial and Labor Relations, Cornell University, Ithaca, N.Y., 1956.

Schurz, William Lytle: *This New World,* E. P. Dutton & Co., Inc., New York, 1954.

Shapiro, Samuel: *Invisible Latin America,* Beacon Press, Boston, 1963.

Silvert, Kalman H.: *The Conflict Society: Reaction and Revolution in Latin America,* The Hauser Press, New Orleans, 1961.

———: *An Invitation to Manipulation,* American Universities Field Staff, Reports Service, New York, 1960.

———: *The Meeting of North and South,* American Universities Field Staff, Reports Service, New York, 1961.

Smith, Earl T.: *The Fourth Floor: An Account of the Castro Communist Revolution,* Random House, Inc., New York, 1962.

Smith, Robert F.: *The U.S. and Cuba: Business and Diplomacy, 1917–1960,* Bookman Associates, New York, 1962.

Special Consultative Committee on Security, *Initial General Report,* Pan American Union, Washington, D.C., 1962.

Stark, Harry: *Social and Economic Frontiers in Latin America,* William C. Brown Company, Dubuque, Iowa, 1961.

Stein, Edwin C.: *Cuba, Castro, and Communism,* MacFadden Publications, Inc., New York, 1962.

Strausz-Hupé, Robert, et al.: *Protracted Conflict,* Harper & Brothers, New York, 1959.

Strengthening of Internal Security, Pan American Union, Washington, D.C., 1953.

Study of Inter-Latin American Trade, United Nations, Department of Public Information, New York, 1957.

Szulc, Tad: *Twilight of the Tyrants,* Holt, Rinehart and Winston, Inc., New York, 1959.

———: *The Winds of Revolution,* Frederick A. Praeger, Inc., New York, 1963.

Tannenbaum, Frank: *Ten Keys to Latin America,* Alfred A. Knopf, Inc., New York, 1963.

Taylor, Wayne C., and John Lindeman: *The Creole Petroleum Corpo-*

ration in Venezuela, National Planning Association, Washington, D.C., 1955.

Thomas, Ann Van Wynen, and A. J. Thomas, Jr.: *Non-Intervention: The Law and its Import in the Americas,* Southern Methodist University Press, Dallas, Tex., 1956.

————: *The Organization of American States,* Southern Methodist University Press, Dallas, Tex., 1963.

Ugarte, Manuel: *The Destiny of a Continent,* Alfred A. Knopf, Inc., New York, 1925.

Ulloa, Alberto: *Derecho internacional público,* vols. II, III, 4th ed., Edicione Iberoamericanas, S.A., Madrid, 1957.

United States Agency for International Development: *Latin American USOMs Seminar on Agrarian Reform,* Feb. 21–24, 1961, Santiago, Chile.

————: *Northeast Survey Report,* 1962.

————: *U.S. Foreign Assistance and Assistance from International Organizations, July 1, 1945–June 30, 1961,* rev. ed., 1962.

U.S. Department of Commerce, Commerce Committee for the Alliance for Progress: *Proposals to Improve the Flow of U.S. Private Investment to Latin America,* 1963.

U.S. Department of Defense, Bureau of Intelligence and Research: *World Strength of the Communist Parties,* 1963.

U.S. Department of State: *Educational and Cultural Diplomacy 1961,* 1962.

————: *Principal U.S. Programs in Latin America in the Fields of Education, Science, and Culture,* 1962.

United States Senate, Subcommittee on American Republics Affairs of the Committee on Foreign Relations, *United States–Latin American Relations,* 86th Cong., 2d Sess., 1960.

Urquidi, Victor L.: *The Challenge of Development in Latin America,* Frederick A. Praeger, Inc., New York, 1964.

————: *Free Trade and Economic Integration in Latin America,* University of California Press, Berkeley, 1962.

————: *Viabilidad económica de América latina,* Fondo de Cultura Económica, Mexico, 1962.

Ward, Barbara: *The Rich Nations and Poor Nations,* W. W. Norton & Company, Inc., New York, 1962.

Whitaker, Arthur P. (ed.): *Latin America and the Enlightenment,* 2d ed., Cornell University Press, Ithaca, N.Y., 1961.

————: *Nationalism in Latin America,* University of Florida Press, Gainesville, Fla., 1962.

————: *The Western Hemisphere Idea*, Cornell University Press, Ithaca, N.Y., 1954.

Whitaker, Urban G., Jr.: *Propaganda and International Relations*, Chandler Publishing Co., San Francisco, 1960.

Wood, Bryce: *The Making of the Good Neighbor Policy*, Columbia University Press, New York, 1961.

Wood, Richardson, and Virginia Keyser: *Sears, Roebuck de México, S.A.*, National Planning Association, Washington, D.C., 1953.

Woytinsky, W. S.: *The U.S. and Latin America's Economy*, The Tamiment Institute, New York, 1958.

Yepes, José María: *Del Congreso de Panamá a la Conferencia de Caracas, 1826–1954*, vol. II, Caracas, 1955.

————: *La Philosophie du panaméricanisme et organisation de la paix*, Editions de la Baconnière, Neuchâtel, 1945.

Index